The *Sales*Mind

SMARTER SELLING. POWERFUL LIVING.

DOUG TRENARY

Doug Trenary's Fast - Track, Inc.
Atlanta, Georgia

Edited by Warren Jamison

10   9   8   7   6   5   4   3   2   1

To my wife, Demetri, the greatest soul mate and cheerleader a man could ever have and who gave me our two wonderful children, Tyler and Blake. You are the light of my life.

Acknowledgments

This book would not have been possible without the contributions of many, many people over many years. I offer to these special people my most sincere thanks. To my clients and many thousands of seminar attendees over the years, I also thank you beyond words. Your feedback and successes are the anvil upon which this book was hammered out. Thank you all for helping me create and stay with the vision of The *Sales*Mind.

Tim Owen----Thank you for showing me with love and excellence how to sell properly in the early days at Lanier when I was so young and green. Those long field days, coaching sessions, and demo practice sessions at night got me started on the right path.

Tom Hopkins----Thank you for providing your classic, timeless sales fundamentals that convinced me why selling is in fact the highest paid hard work in the world— and the lowest paid easy work. There has never been a more effective skills author and coach.

Warren Jamison----Thank you for your masterful editing and diligence in molding my vision into a powerful and fun work.

Demetri Trenary----Thank you for the objective insight to spend night after night crafting the words to have just the right meaning. You will never understand fully your contribution.

The Team----Thank you to all the committed staff and partners over the years who helped run a successful business wherever I may have been.

The Customer----Thank you, whoever you are and have been since 1983, for the opportunity to serve. There is nothing to contribute without you.

CONTENTS

Preface   vi
Introduction   viii

Part I: DESIRE: Leveraging Yourself   **1**

1 Focus: The *Concentration* of Desire   3
2 Purpose: The *Motive* of Desire   25
3 Action: The *Execution* of Desire   51
4 Response: The *Test* of Desire   69

Part II: PERSUASION: Leveraging Buyers   **87**

5 Connection: The *Pathway* of Persuasion   91
6 Value: The *Engine* of Persuasion   111
7 Urgency: The *Effect* of Persuasion   133
8 Leverage: The *Price* of Persuasion   153

Part III: Timing: Leveraging Time   **181**

9 Priority: The *Object* of Timing   183
10 Control: The *Flow* of Timing   201
11 Coverage: The *Scope* of Timing   221
12 Adjustment: The *Change* of Timing   239

Afterword   261
About the Author   263

Preface

During 1995, I wrote down and typed massive amounts of information, patterns, and experiences dedicated toward answering one question. This question was an obsession with me, a critical point in my selling and training career that consumed me. The question was, "What do the best sales professionals do every day?"

I wanted desperately to create an accurate profile of these achievers so that I could share it in my seminars and ultimately in this book. Not only had I been a professional sales trainer and consultant for over ten years and sold since 1983, but I had also accumulated boxes of notes and filled scores of legal pads with writing and outlines in my pursuit. I instructed my mind every day to identify the core traits of the sales elite.

Never underestimate the power of the mind when you pour in data with urgency, seeking answers. About 2 a.m. on the morning of December 5, 1995, I awoke from a sound sleep with an absolutely crystal-clear outline of The *Sales*Mind elements. I could "see" in my mind's eye the *exact* twelve elements *in order* of the success profile I had been seeking. My wife thought I was crazy, but I zoomed downstairs, flipped on my computer, and typed out the outline exactly as you see it today. The words had been presented to my mind as if sent to me in a letter.

Over the next eight years, I persistently crafted and adjusted the content of The *Sales*Mind. I did this while training and traveling all over North America presenting this profile for development and feedback to thousands of business owners, managers, and salespeople from every walk of life. These people were of every experience level, and they sold every conceivable product or service.

My clients have sold tens of millions of dollars by applying its power. The book continued to evolve and gel. I never, ever wanted to just author *any* sales book, because the bookshelves are full of classics. My goal was to put forth a unique perspective of sales success that would make a difference—one that was absolutely proven to produce sales income to the highest degree, period. It has, and here it is for you.

I now offer you today the highest level of refinement of The *Sales*Mind. Enjoy and use its power in your life.

Introduction

What is a "*Sales*Mind?"

One crucial law of success is to establish a winning *position*. Consider the game of golf. You may play golf and even play well. There are also professionals who play golf. Then there is Tiger Woods. He is the master at getting in position to win and then winning! Just ask his opponents.

The *Sales*Mind is the Tiger Woods of Sales. Not just a salesperson, not just a professional, *Sales*Minds are experts at selling from positions of strength. They are to sales what Edison is to inventors, or Einstein to physics. The *Sales*Mind is the *Sales Master*.

At the core of their mastery is the knowledge that success does not happen with just *any* position. Maximum results in life or business require a position of *leverage*, or positional advantage. However, any relationship position carrying an advantage must also be earned. The *Sales*Mind knows how to earn and establish a leverage position within the relationships of life and business. They most certainly know how to establish a leverage position in a transaction with customers, whom I call "buyers" in this book (to emphasize their active, purchasing role). And best of all, *your* buyers will gain maximum benefit from this type of relationship!

How do You Establish Positive Relationship Positions?

My years of research and experience tell me that sales success is based on the position of three key relationships I have named:

"The Desire Relationship." How you relate to *Yourself.*

"The Persuasion Relationship." How you relate to *Buyers*.

"The Timing Relationship." How you relate to *Time.*

Each individual relationship involves you. You with yourself, you with buyers, and you with time. All three relationships also interact with each other: Desire with persuasion, persuasion with timing, and so on. All three individual *Sales*Mind relationships are interconnected, and they comprise the entire perspective from which this book was written.

Why Should *You* be a *Sales*Mind?

The *Sales*Mind defines twelve powerful laws to help you immediately establish a leverage position with Yourself, with Buyers, and with Time. You will also have a stronger foundation of excellence on which all of your selling skills can grow.

You will offer more sincere service, feel better physically and emotionally, and make the most money possible with your available time. Your level of thinking will be higher, your fundamentals sharper, and your principles more powerful.

Everyone today is looking for a system that delivers faster and more profitable sales results. This book is that system!

PART I: DESIRE

LEVERAGING YOURSELF

D esire often is easy to see in others but can be hard to sustain in ourselves. We observe great performers achieve phenomenal results and see clearly that a strong desire to achieve is behind their performance. And it is.

But in a world that is increasingly stressful, how do you sustain desire?

By anchoring motives that are God-inspired and then establishing *a successful relationship with yourself.* In other words, you must have a successful personal relationship position.

To acquire that position, the positive side of you must out-leverage the negative side of you. Your passions have to outmuscle your fears.

THE MISSION OF THE NEXT FOUR CHAPTERS IS TO HELP YOU ESTABLISH A POSITIVE LEVERAGE POSITION WITH YOURSELF.

In hot pursuit of that goal, the SalesMind answers these interlocking questions about desire:

- **Focus (Chapter 1): How do you sustain the *concentration* of your desires?**

- **Purpose (Chapter 2): What are the *motives* of your desires?**

- **Action (Chapter 3): How do you *execute* your desires?**

- **Response (Chapter 4): How do you react to the *testing* of your desires?**

Leveraging your achievement position is always the first step of greatness. These are life skills. They apply to any endeavor.

If you have the drive, motivation, and persistence to succeed, you'll want to hone your skills to achieve maximum impact.

How quickly—even whether—you reach maximum impact and win its high income depends on how thoroughly you train yourself for the success that can be yours.

The tools you need to do so are in this book.

1

FOCUS

THE LASER BEAM OF SUCCESS

An eagle high in a tree scans for food far below and sees two rabbits. The eagle knows that if he chases two rabbits both will escape. So he focuses in on *one*, and goes in for the kill.

You are driving safely through your subdivision when you notice a squirrel start across the street and reach half way. As you get close, he senses your car approaching, gets distracted, scrambles left to right, and ends up a grease spot on the pavement. You assumed he would just continue safely forward to the other side and could not avoid him.

Are you an eagle or a squirrel? Do you zero in on what is important in sales and life or become easily confused and distracted?

In life today, our senses are flooded with a continuous battle for our attention from TV, finances, families, phones, computers, pressures, and traffic. How do we sort it all out? Perhaps the most difficult challenge of all in today's complex world is to establish the consistent pattern of defining the most important pursuits that embody truth and meaning, and then giving those thoughts and tasks maximum attention.

> *"One word of truth outweighs the whole world."*
> —— **Alexander Solzhenitsyn**

FOCUS IS THE CONCENTRATION OF DESIRE

Focus is defined as "adjustment for distinctness or clarity." And a *Sales*Mind establishes these distinct behaviors involving their own focus:

- How to be clear in their thoughts.
- How to concentrate and sustain that concentration.
- How to identify, formulate, intensify, analyze and strengthen mental specifics.
- What to be clear about that has purpose, creates results, and has value.

- How to place their unguarded attention on what they have clarified.
- How to fertilize desire, which must sustain itself against resistance in the pressures, challenges, and setbacks of life.

Concentration skills are so crucial because although the subject matter of concentration will constantly change, the process of concentration will not. A *Sales*Mind develops the ability to command intense concentration on *any* subject. This becomes an enormously powerful mental tool that tends to grow stronger the more it is used.

Aim specific activities at achieving your most important objectives. Leverage your focus into contributions and results. Maintain perspective on what to focus on. These mental habits are constant with *Sales*Minds.

Focus is the launching pad for all powerful business and personal success. All other *Sales*Mind skills rely on focus.

Focus Power Rests on Two Simple Relationships:

One: If you concentrate on positives, you place yourself in a position where positive outcomes dominate or have leverage.

Two: If you concentrate on negatives, you place yourself in a position where negative outcomes dominate or have leverage.

KEY: To "place yourself in a position" is to set up an outcome, bad or good. *Leverage* is the active state of which outcome (positive or negative) is more dominant.

Do You Benefit from Proper Focus?

Absolutely. Scientific study shows the positive effect of focusing on challenging activity as we age. For example:

Mental focus grows membrane specifically for synapses where nerve cells connect and talk to each other—thus improving memory and mental acuity in general.

Physical focus with activity supplies more blood and nutrients to brain cells to keep them healthier, and supplies growth hormone to keep existing brain cells alive longer.

Mental and physical activity helps keep you healthy. JUST DO IT!

*A Sales**Mind** produces the highest possible mental, emotional, physical, and financial results by first understanding the power of effective concentration.*

YOU HAVE TWO FOCUS TASKS

Remember, the *Sales*Mind is the *Sales Master*. Individuals who have gained *Sales*Mind status have highly successful relationships with themselves, with buyers, and with time. They know how to focus. Everyone says, "You have to focus." Well, no kidding. But more specifically, as a *Sales*Mind you basically face two tasks or challenges relating to focus:

Mastering your own focus. This chapter deals primarily with this issue. A *Sales*Mind must be able to initiate, sustain, and finalize a focal point or issue. Without personal focus, there is no way to stay on the message of determining and providing customer value.

Getting the buyer to focus on your product or service. This is especially difficult in today's crowded business world. Our present environment of mass information has reduced a normal person's (the average buyer's) attention span for absorbing a presentation from twenty minutes down to ten minutes. Chapters 4 through 6 will deal with this issue. If you can't attract and sustain the *buyer's* focus on the value of your program, they will not buy it, period. It won't matter if *you* only have focus. It's a dual challenge.

SalesMinds harness the skills of focus to direct their own attention as well as the attention of the buyer.

HOW DO YOU FOCUS NOW?

Michael Jordan practiced diligently for years on the craft of basketball and set goals to add new layers to his game each season **(time)**. He compared his skills, attitudes, and work habits to others on the court, to the great past players of the game, and to the time-tested principles of winning **(perspective)**.

Every summer, he relentlessly watched prior season video to pick out little imperfections in his game, a dribble here, and a piece of footwork there **(study)**. He then worked repetitiously hour after hour on the court practicing to improve those details **(training)**. In the final moments of big games, he had the guts to want the ball, got it, and hit the historical clinchers to win championships **(pressure)**.

It is this synergy of elements that made him one of the most focused performers ever in any walk of life. Focus is the *laser beam of success*! Every *Sales*Mind should be ecstatic about their mind's ability to concentrate on performance and its benefits. It's incredibly valuable.

But it's impossible to take a new focus detour of improvement until you know the road you're on now. Over time, you have developed a certain level of ability to isolate and tighten thoughts and emotions to generate action. That ability is based on your handling of a number of variables that have accumulated over your life. The same variables Michael Jordan successfully mastered.

In Sales, Be Like Mike

Time

How old you are does determine how many *total* experiences in life you've had. However, age is not the measure of your wisdom. Some people are chronologically old and young in experience because they don't build knowledge.

Others are chronologically young at 25 but already old in experience. The latter is a priceless state that comes from analyzing each year's experience and the resulting outcomes, and quickly building another valuable layer of knowledge on that experience.

Perspective

You have built your own unique viewpoint, the angle from which you see everything. How have you compared, contrasted, and patterned your life experiences? How many comparisons have you made between your experiences and success principles? Have you simply had experiences and let them pass? Or have you evaluated those experiences, searching for meanings and patterns, strengths and weaknesses, and for positives to build on and negatives to avoid?

Study

How much total time and intense thought on any single issue have you invested for the purpose of mastering that specific piece of knowledge? How much information have you found, studied, made notes on, torn down, built up, and organized to imbed it in your mind?

Training

How much training and practice on a skill have you experienced to intensify your ability to evaluate, expand on, and execute all angles of that skill with confidence in any circumstance?

Pressure

How much courageous action have you taken over time in real pressure situations where money is on the line? How many times have you been successful under pressure?

Pressure where success or failure is on the line creates high focus. High focus on a repetitive basis leads to mastery of skills. Your current state of focus skill is not simply a mental function. It is a *behavior* of concentration that is compounded from a history of study and action under pressure.

External and Internal Focus

Do you focus more on the outside world for direction, or more on your own thoughts and dreams for direction? This is a question with enormous implications. As humans, we naturally either run from pain or move toward pleasure. Our experiences and perceptions of those pains and pleasures can determine the direction of our focus.

All people focus in a combination of two dimensions to direct their behaviors and character. I call this "focus blend." The blend is the ratio of external to internal focus time, and one type normally dominates the other. Let's look at these two personality types:

EXTERNALS

This type of person, in whom external focus dominates, is conditioned to a higher percentage of external focus time, which is centered on the absorption of outside stimuli obtained from their senses, mostly sight and hearing. Their reliance is focused on the influences and people outside of themselves for feedback and direction. There are two primary effects as a result of external focus:

Constructive: Your external focus is empowering when it is centered on the expression of worship, on the absorption of new learning, or on interacting with positive people and role models. It is also invaluable when evaluating the world around you for the purpose of understanding patterns and supporting your goals.

Destructive: But, when you have no mental and emotional filters of concrete beliefs, values, and goals to sort out the effect of life's many influences, this type of focus makes you vulnerable to the outside world's direction. That's a scary proposition with media, peer pressure, and the Internet. It's really scary for your kids.

INTERNALS

This type of person, in whom internal focus dominates, is conditioned to a higher percentage of internal focus time. This focus time is divided between two important functions (a) the generation of predetermined, positive, organized thoughts to create an internal mental framework of great efficiency and resiliency, and (b) the creation and maintenance of a "filter system" to eliminate harmful outside influences while admitting wholesome and helpful ideas and information.

"Filters" are sets of instructions strong-willed people set up in their minds to protect their thinking, which they center on their dreams, values, goals, and contributions. These filter systems allow them to pull what they need to nourish their thoughts and feelings from outside influences. There are also two primary effects as a result of internal focus:

Constructive: Your internal focus is enriching when it serves as a constructive framework for your thoughts and emotions. Properly exercised, this type of focus enables you to carve your path through the outside world, using its influences to help you navigate to your goals.

Destructive: But, internal focus becomes destructive when it descends into narcissism, self-centeredness, and excessive self-absorption. Good thinking, concentration skills, and effective emotional management are not designed to seal you off as an island unto yourself.

> *"Self-examination is healthy but self-absorption is not; self-correction is a winner but self-flagellation is a sure loser."*
> —— **William Safire**
> Syndicated New York Times columnist

What Is Your Ratio of External to Internal Focus?

As a rule, make sure that internal focus is your *dominant* system. That way you are accountable to your own thinking. But, do you need to examine and make adjustments to decrease/increase your external focus?

Do you need to increase/decrease your internal focus? Think of any truly high achiever, whether that person is a super *Sales*Mind, a great athlete, mother, businessperson, coach, or historical leader.

They have developed the clear skills of managing the constructive/destructive balance of when to look out and when to look in, with the primary strength of looking in.

Let's take a special look at those people who have developed masterful internal focus skills.

Strong Internal Focusers Know:

- How to generate focus into a positive emotional state of mind.
- How to narrow what to focus on and identify what not to focus on.
- How to intensify their focus on what they are seeking or doing.
- How to convert a state of focus into decision and action.
- How to enlarge their focus to keep things in perspective.
- How to recognize and immediately shift out of a negative focus.

***Sales*Minds** *first gain an in-depth understanding of how they focus now. Then they use that knowledge to carefully balance their external/internal focus to reach the best mix to speed them toward their goals.*

MASTER YOUR FOCUS SKILLS

Do you have control of your incredibly powerful ability to focus? You will have that mental control when you have mastered your capabilities to:

- Strengthen or change your immediate focus.
- Intensify positive emotions that empower you.
- Diminish negative emotions that paralyze you.
- Change your negative emotions to positive.

Strengthen or Change Your Immediate Focus

Let's start by concentrating on specific actions to strengthen your focus skills at any given moment:

Change your language. Changing language and verbal communication *instantly* has an effect on emotion.

First, change your internal language or self-talk by writing down and then conditioning affirmations of positive success.

Second, make a daily commitment to a new verbal language reflecting your new image of success and possibility.

Third, change that language by changing physical words, adjusting, deleting, and changing context. For example, "should" to "must," "can't" to "can," "might" to "will."

Understand that you use two languages, internal and external. You can say internally that you love someone, while externally you don't communicate that love. Work to align your languages in a positive manner.

Do something physical. When you do, your mental state and posture will automatically shift to concentrate on those physical demands. Deal with your worries while running, riding a bike, walking, lifting weights, or engaging in competitive sports to shift your emotional focus.

Question and answer a key topic on paper. Seek out five specific written answers to a well-defined question such as, "How can I learn computers?" This type of specific question will compel you to find focused answers.

Detail-out your topic. Again, do this on paper or on a computer, and keep an ongoing notebook or journal.

Interact with someone. Share ideas or topics that demand open-ended and interactive conversations. Talk out problems and ideas. The mind will shift emotionally to the new topic and/or person. Get a different perspective.

Change the sensory stimulants of your current environment. Pick up a book to read, listen to music, raise the blinds, open a window, turn on a bright light, and so on.

Change your sensory stimulants by moving physically to another place. Make another sales call in person. Imagine that! Take a walk, a trip, a vacation, change rooms, get up and walk out into the sun. All these activities help you change focus.

Pray or meditate to change focus. Purge your stressful thoughts to relax brain activity. Harvard medical school recently did a study and reports that praying and focusing away from stressful thoughts can lower brain wave activity, heart rate, blood pressure, and can even increase fertility (fertility increased in 40 percent of married couples studied). That's powerful stuff.

Change or strengthen your thinking in two ways:
  First, generate greater *quantity* of thinking by simply accumulating more information.
  Second, generate greater *quality* of thinking through better handling of information: Question. Read. Interview. Structure. Sequence. Distill. Prioritize. Communicate. Compare. Validate. Justify. Computerize.

Constantly train and retrain to learn and reinforce. Repetition of focus creates conditioning of proper thought patterns and skills.

Remain practical. Learn to develop and apply these skills on a practical day-to-day basis.

Positive Emotions Empower You—Intensify Them and Live Longer

  Only humans were given this conscious capacity. Research shows a positive emotional outlook can also help you live longer. A recent study conducted by Yale University and reported in the *Journal of Personality and Social Psychology* shows that in 660 men and women over age 50 followed for 23 years, those respondents who reported having a positive attitude toward aging lived an average of more than seven years longer than those who had a more dismal view of getting older.

"How one feels about getting old is more important even than having low blood pressure or cholesterol," said Becca Levy of Yale. In our world, that means you can have longer to sell!

A big part of that positive emotional management is how you review past positive experiences. In the brain, positive (or negative) emotions are linked or associated to past images, sounds, sensations, and experiences and then are stored in the brain.

To intensify a positive emotion, focus and "call up" (as a computer does) a beginning past good experience, which might be a grainy image or sound that you would like to re-experience. Then hold that image. Replay in your mind a great beach trip, the love of your parents, the first steps of your child, or a great song in high school. Generate emotion!

Then concentrate and intensify that image or sound until it becomes a clear, prevalent state of mind. You will then be able re-create those same positive emotions instantly whenever needed. This type of positive mindset serves as the emotional fuel for your sales efforts.

When you can do this type of instant exercise as a daily habit amidst the turmoil of life, success awaits you! Emotions empower human behavior, and selling is one form of that behavior.

Finally, write down an emotional inventory of the good feelings you want to experience daily for thirty days in a diary. For these positive emotions, mentally color in the circumstances, things, people, hobbies, and so on that make you feel the very best whether you are presently in that situation or simply reflecting on it. Get photos, cut out magazine pictures, and make diagrams of anything that supports these images.

The key is to *imbed* these images so deeply in your mind that they can be called up clearly and at will when you are in a negative emotional state. This is the process of intensifying positive focus, and it will have a wonderful effect on you. You might:

- Play or sing your favorite songs.
- Do something from your past like touch a baseball bat.
- Look up and think of the awesome power of the sun.
- Read positive stories with victories or great personal achievements.
- Pray every day and meditate about good outcomes like the birth of your child.
- Replay a great vacation with your spouse or school friends.
- Remember a tough victory like a very hard test or major sales push at the office.

*Sales*Minds need to lock a vault packed with positive images in their brains, the contents of which they can call upon to emotionally empower themselves to overcome each day's challenges.

"Finally brothers, whatever is true, whatever is noble, whatever is right, whatever is pure, whatever is lovely, whatever is admirable—if anything is excellent or praiseworthy—think about such things."
—— **Philippians 4:8**

Diminish the Negative Emotions That Paralyze You

In reverse, a *Sales*Mind has to *reduce* the effect of negative emotion on their life and sales efforts. You will benefit greatly if you will do these four things in sequence to lessen the impact of any negative emotion:

1. *Clarify your negative emotions in writing.* Once you have that first list of bad feelings that you have experienced in the past, make a commitment to deal with the *source* of each emotion. You might talk with someone who was involved in the bad feeling, or go to a location to relive an experience. Then think through how you can resolve, challenge, and communicate to diminish the feeling's power.

2. *Carry out a first action at a negative emotion.* Take one first small step and attack the emotion. For example, address cold-call fear with the action of five immediate phone or in-person calls. Those actions will always diminish fear because the fear is only imagined. If you have larger life fears like the fear of poverty or the fear of criticism, address those fears with daily, bold action to allow your courage, achievements, and beliefs to be your dominant focus.

**3.   *Continue to weaken the emotion with sustained*
action.** Consistent positive action will recondition the mind
and weaken a negative emotion. For example, you might
desire to reduce a past guilt, like poor grades in school.
Take action and enlist in a program to help illiterate adults
read. They have a lot more guilt than you ever had. There
are plenty of people like this who need your help. By
helping them, *your* guilt is diminished. Sustained action
also helps develop a wider perspective around these
negative emotions to put them in their proper place and
reduce their intensity. When they are in perspective, their
power diminishes.

4.   *Convert the emotion to a positive strength.* See
your sustained actions through in a systematic, planned
way. When you complete a goal, you turn that former
negative emotional weakness into a current source of
positive emotional strength.

After a Super Bowl victory, Dallas Cowboys owner
Jerry Jones was asked how the Cowboys got through the
intense criticism they received during the season. He said,
"We decided to focus on the positives (to perform) instead
of on the negatives." Successful people have a pattern of
thinking and saying things of this nature.

Change Negative Focus to Positive

A recent survey conducted by the New York-based
Conference Board of 5000 people, found that only 51
percent of Americans were happy with their jobs. Does that
mean a whopping 49 percent are varying degrees of
unhappy? No wonder everybody looks so angry on the

highway during the morning rush hour, and will kill you on the road to get home at night. When I hear survey responses like this, I wonder if these unhappy workers need to simply change their unhappiness mindset (no matter what the job) to one of, "I choose to be happy no matter what." You can't be happy until you change your focus to *happiness*.

However, a *Sales*Mind knows how to change a negative mindset to a positive one instantly, consciously, and systematically by changing their focus from negative to positive. For a *Sales*Mind, this change may be a change from negative self-pity or fears about selling to a positive mindset that focuses instead on the purpose of how and why to serve buyers.

This mental habit of *instant emotional conversion* is incredibly valuable to the sales professional to make the most of each positive moment in a day. Long periods of hesitation, worry, and distraction kill productivity. Control what you focus on, and that will control the accompanying feelings you experience. Feelings help drive your actions, which in turn, determine your results. You must also be consistent at remembering the right things about your life. Focus and....

- Remember who you are.
- Remember that you have done it before.
- Remember it's no big deal (in your life).
- Remember "this too shall pass" (for pain).
- Remember the plight of others in relation to your own situation.
- Remember what you want and the price you're willing to pay for it.

"I know God won't give me anything I can't handle. I just wish He wouldn't trust me so much."
—— **Mother Teresa**

SalesMinds *effectively operate their mindsets so that positive emotions dominate and create positive behavior.*

WHAT SHOULD YOU FOCUS ON?

Start answering today these life questions involving:

- **Possibility:** What are you truly capable of?
- **Pattern:** What are your consistent choices of time use?
- **Purpose:** What really has the most value in this situation or in my life?
- **Priority:** What is truly important at this instant?
- **Positives:** What are the good aspects of this situation?
- **Passion:** How do I generate a powerful, positive emotional response?
- **Precision:** How can I have clarity, detail, definition, and accuracy in my thoughts?
- **Performance:** How can I take action now?
- **Process:** What are the pieces, sequences, and steps?

- **Physical:** How can I generate results from physical posture and exercise?
- **Partnering:** How can I cooperate with someone else in a given circumstance?

Again, sit down and start answering these questions in writing. Answer them whenever you are planning or beginning a new task. Make this asking and answering a habitual pattern. The answers will concentrate your thoughts toward a clear and powerful result.

*Sales*Minds *become what they focus on most!*

Focus is the *concentration* of desire. It is the ability to sustain specific thoughts and positive emotions in a world of distractions. But on what issues of worth and purpose do you consistently place your focus? The search for those answers beckons our call.

2

PURPOSE

A REASON TO PAY THE PRICE

W hat drives you deep inside your heart? What is your true passion? What is your number one reason to live? As you reflect on those answers, consider these historical facts about people who found their true passions and lived, or are living, outstanding lives that brought, or are bringing, them great satisfaction:

- For decades, Mother Teresa immersed herself in Calcutta's miserable slums to help the poorest of the poor.

The Apostle Paul endured beatings, hunger, isolation, and abandonment to spread the Gospel into the Greek world of around 40-70 A.D.

Henry Ford knew that engineering the V-8 engine was possible even after hearing his engineers repeatedly assert that it was impossible.

As a youth, Pete Maravich often practiced basketball for eight or nine hours a day. This self-imposed discipline enabled him to crush the all-time collegiate scoring career record, averaging over 44 points a game for four straight seasons (although his incredible total only represents *three* seasons because freshman NCAA statistics were not counted at that time).

Responding to 9/11, President George W. Bush put into motion the most sweeping financial, political, and military campaign ever to root out terrorism around the world.

Working Moms and Dads get up early every day, endure traffic and fatigue, give up their time, and hustle to give their kids the opportunity to achieve.

What do these and other successful people of different circumstances have in common?

Purpose. They have a passionate focus on missions greater than themselves. They possess the habit of keeping their minds on what is valuable beyond the hurricane of the day.

Why do you sell? What is the money for? Why do you really do what you do? What reasons are you paying the price for? I mean, *really* paying the price?

As a *Sales*Mind—that is, a professional *Sales Master*—is your purpose a factor in your sales life?

Absolutely. When salespeople do not have purpose, they will instead have a state of indecision and vagueness that leads to frustration, disappointment and, in some cases, laziness. Under any such scenario, sales will be far short of those made by someone with a strong drive to accomplish their purpose.

Let's say you have a major financial setback and go bankrupt. Or there is a sudden death in your family, or you are slammed down by illness. Unfortunately, it often takes a fall into one of life's deep canyons to impel many people to start facing questions about their purpose in life.

Don't wait until you fall off a cliff to really focus on your mission. Take a more positive approach. Ask yourself today, whatever your circumstances at the moment, this question:

"What is my purpose?"

You will also notice early in this book that what I desire for you is not merely to have a purpose, but to have the *right* purpose.

PURPOSE IS THE MOTIVE OF DESIRE

Purpose is defined as "a result or effect that is intended or desired with determination or resolve." *Sales*Minds focus on purposes of deep importance that are able to motivate them. Their purpose is the reason for their effort. A *Sales*Mind will always sell more when they have driving, intentional motives fueling their mission, such concepts as serving and caring for others.

> *"It saddens me how many people go through life*
> *without a focus on a purpose."*
> —— **Frank Gifford,** the New York Giants football
> Hall-of-Famer, in an interview about his career.

*Sales*Minds define what they consistently choose to focus on and why. Those definitions are their purpose, and a strong, specific purpose will leverage the desire to achieve. Ask yourself these two vital questions:

"Is there a moral connotation to my purpose?"

"Is it really my purpose and not one taken on to please someone else?"

Unfortunately, purposes do not require a moral floor, as exemplified by Charles Manson, Jim Jones, Adolph Hitler, Usama Bin Laden, and many other lesser fanatics, serial killers, and psychopaths. Certainly all four of the monsters named above had—or have—purposes.

What if your purpose is to party, eat too much of the wrong things, and just feel good? What if your purpose is just to make as much money as you can instead of making as much of a difference in other's lives as you can?

To maximize your life's achievements, question yourself deeply about your motives and desires.

What Is Your Purpose?

Is my purpose harmful to others, including buyers, in any way?

Is my purpose selfish and inconsiderate of others I care for?

Is my purpose emotionally gratifying in the short term but positioned for long-term disaster?

Is my purpose an investment in my life and the lives of others, or is it merely to increase present consumption?

Is my purpose of sufficient strength to withstand massive pain, pressure, and criticism?

Is my purpose in line with my talents?

Is my purpose a powerful fuel for my sales and business life?

Is my purpose worth the commitment of time and energy it demands?

Is my purpose worth sharing with others, including my buyers?

Does God inspire my purpose in any way, or am I just operating on my own free will?

These questions are just the tip of the iceberg of understanding the power of purpose. Purpose should be a deep spiritual, philosophical, and emotional trough to drink from. Is it for you?

Pay Attention

The success of their *lives* (partly expressed through their occupation of selling) is what motivates *Sales*Minds and is what has the most meaning for them. The *Sales*Mind operates most effectively when functioning within the specific meaningful framework of a defined set of desires.

Your desires are part of what you pay attention to. (The other attention-getters are your pains). Your desire to help buyers and achieve sales success is the energy of the sales effort from your perspective.

When you channel these desires and energies through a set of mental filters (your experiences and beliefs), they accelerate in the right direction. That direction should be toward your buyers' best interests as well as toward the realization of the dreams and plans that are your goals. Your purpose should be like the explosion in a rifle that channels a bullet through a barrel and sends it toward a target.

- The gunpowder is your purpose.
- The barrel of the rifle is your belief system.
- The bullet is your daily action.
- The target is your goal.

Why do *Sales*Minds need to have all these elements firing properly in their rifles? The reason is that every day places difficulties in the path of taking the necessary actions so that you can move in a positive and profitable direction.

Many kinds of obstacles such as frustration, disappointment, hesitation, reluctance, and rejection—not to mention car trouble, bad roads, storms, and other physical barriers to progress—will challenge one's determination.

These negative forces will consistently swallow individuals who lack the right purpose as an effective counter-force. You might also think of purpose as *character with drive.*

So, to accelerate past the negatives, a *Sales*Mind is driven by six congruent elements of purpose:

Service
Balance
Identity
Beliefs
Values
Goals

Next, we'll examine how each of these elements is a special dimension of purpose.

*A **Sales**Mind gains purpose by developing strong motives that can withstand the massive resistance of today's marketplace.*

SERVICE AND PURPOSE

I will— Your first and most important purpose as a *Sales*Mind is to render service. Even if you have no goals or passions in your sales life (how is this possible?) you have to possess at least a service mindset toward satisfying your buyer.

Do you really care about the success and welfare of your buyers? If you got paid the same without extra service, would you render your best service effort anyway? Your constant focus is always on the buyer's welfare, which is not always easy to do because buyers can be demanding, inconsistent, and untruthful. But why are you in business? You are in business to *provide value* to buyers, and then, in turn, to be compensated.

Your purpose in life has to be congruent with and supportive of this objective. Your focus has to remain on the buyer's needs, whether in-person or not. Remember, service is not a generalization; it's both a mindset and an action. Oftentimes in an account, you have to look for a person to serve. Service involves helping people, one at a time, with intent and action. This variable will ultimately determine the buyer's perception of you, thus affecting your success.

A *Sales*Mind lives by, "Serve and the money will follow." This reverent creed is easily tossed out by sales managers and authors as being easier said than done, and is a hangover from an earlier, less competitive era. When most salespeople are making an average income and stretching it to get ahead, it's not easy to look through the ultra-pure lens of "service first" because their own struggle keeps getting in the way. Yet, to repeat, "service first" is the most important attitude in selling, from first contact to furthering buyer relationships. Your income simply has to be seen as a by-product of serving, helping, and giving something of value.

Principles of Service

*Sales*Minds can rely on these service truths:

- Buyers will test your sincerity. Rise to the occasion. Respond early and precisely.
- Find a service model you can study that will show you the most effective and efficient methods of

executing service as a company, department, or an individual.

- Don't over-promise or stretch claims because you represent all the employees in your company who may serve the buyer, not just yourself.
- Gather as much information as possible so you know how to serve.
- Understand that proactive service costs a lot less than reactive service.
- Keep your buyers. Studies show that finding new customers is at least seven times as expensive and time-consuming as keeping old customers by serving them well.
- Know the difference between expected service and the unexpected service that pleases.

Sequence of Service

In a service situation, a *Sales*Mind must do these three things in order:

1. **Respond immediately** with a "Band-Aid" (an immediate call-back or temporary solution) to eliminate hostility in complaint situations. A quick reaction is critical.
2. **Immediately align** and orchestrate everyone in your company with lots of communication in a planned, hopefully long-term, solution with the buyer.
3. **Confirm satisfaction** with your buyer, preferably in writing.

*"Never lose a customer. Ever since I was a
teenager delivering newspapers, I treated each one like the
most important person in the world. The key to succeeding,
I would learn later, is to take care of the customer."*
—— **Truett Cathy**, founder of
Chick-fil-A Restaurants
(Sales increases for 34 straight years)

A Service Oath to Live by:

The *Sales*Mind promise: "I will always pursue all
elements of the truth with my buyers, even when it hurts to
confront it. My buyer is first human, and therefore
emotional. So the damage of negative emotion directed at
me is never worth the benefit of my lack of service effort. I
see service as a character opportunity and a good selling
investment because both good and bad news travels fast. I
will serve with the attitude that my buyer's welfare shall be
treated exactly as if roles were reversed, and then some."

A job description in any detail can never be
sufficient to describe the willing little extra that elevates a
*Sales*Mind to servant. The *Sales*Mind embodies the servant
attitude. He or she is a servant leader.

***Sales*Minds *exist for the purpose of using desire to
give service.***

BALANCE AND PURPOSE

I flex... One's purpose in life has to be balanced
because, as all *Sales*Minds know, every person is multi-
dimensional in these areas of their lives:

- Family
- Professional/financial
- Social
- Physical
- Educational
- Spiritual

All Derivatives of Purpose Involve Balance

Our examination of the power of having purpose is structured in a balanced system and progression of:

- **Identities:** You are multi-faceted as to who you are.
- **Beliefs:** You believe many things.
- **Values:** You establish an array of priorities.
- **Goals:** You pursue a matrix of achievements.

Being in harmony and consistently balanced in life is very elusive in today's hectic living. How many times have you said, "This year I'm going to get in to shape, make more money . . . " Most people's biggest complaint is "no time." But I contend the lack of balance is also a lack of planning, effort, and discipline. If you don't value balance in your life, you won't work on it. If you don't plan it on paper, you won't realize it. Balancing life is a batting average with a success rate, not a perfect fit of pieces. The positive fact is, balanced people enjoy their daily lives more, manage all aspects of their gains and pains better, and are far more appealing to be with than tunnel-visioned-burnouts. Balanced people have more dimensions and generate more influence.

Many benefits accrue when you harness some proactive control about the daily events in your whole life and acknowledge how they work together in harmony. More benefits follow when you examine how and at what times your life areas, by failing to work together, create conflict and friction. To give you more energy, work on your balance. This will enable you to monitor your priorities better, and build more quality into your daily life. By so doing, you will develop a greater ability to bounce back when one or more area suffers a hard time. This happens automatically because when your life is balanced, you always have smoothly running areas to absorb the shock of the ones in trouble. This results in a more optimistic attitude, and lowers stress. Not a bad way to live.

Ask Yourself Some Balance Questions

- Am I aware of the segmented but unified areas in my own life?
- Do I have some perspective of how each life area relates to the performance of all of the others?
- Do I need to take some immediate action steps to get some momentum going again in one given area that I have been neglecting?
- Do I need to define on paper a plan involving sub-areas or parts of extended family, financial specialties, or specific career desires?

SalesMinds gain greater purpose by balancing and fulfilling multiple desires in their lives.

IDENTITY AND PURPOSE

I am... Who are you? How would you identify yourself if you were asked? How many different (and balanced) ways would you describe who you are? Do your various identities (in our balance categories) have anything to do with your purpose? Yes, your identity and purpose are closely linked. Identity lies at the core of purpose because identity is both how you see yourself and how others see you.

A Clear Identity

Develop and sustain absolute clarity about your own identity:

First, your **Current Identity** is your best present assessment and personal inventory of your strengths and weaknesses in terms of skills, background, associations, talents, experience, knowledge of specifics, affiliations, physical condition, habits, behaviors, emotional tendencies, and even oddities. In addition, it is an honest self-evaluation of your spiritual, family, professional, social, physical, and educational lives.

These identities serve as a powerful self-examination and generate deep thinking about who you are in life at the present time. *Sales*Minds always want a grounded sense of who they are now so they can continuously develop into who they want to be.

Second, your **Desired Identity** is the personality you *want to be* as expressed through the achievement of your goals that support your value system, or the things that are really important to you in life. Your desired identities also span all of the areas of your life, not just business.

You could focus on, "As a family man I'd like to be remembered for . . . or as a physical man I'd like to be known for . . . or when people observe me in my spiritual life I believe they'll see..." Your desired identity should mentally associate with positive role models and character traits you desire to possess; equally important, it should also disassociate or focus away from the influences of negative people or aspects of life that you do not want in your identity.

Write down the six life categories and two headings as I've done on the next page. Then add the words or phrases you believe best describe who you are now, that is, your current identities. On the right side of that same paper, across from the categories and words of your current identity, write down the words or phrases that describe who you want to be in that same life area, that is, your desired identities. I've placed in some arbitrary examples.

Current Identities *and* *Desired Identities*

Social
No active close friendships

Poor people skills

Social
Often spend time with
close friends
Relaxed, confident with
people

Physical
No regular exercise

Lifestyle risks high blood pressure

Sedentary/high cholesterol

Physical
Various regular exercise
routines
Runner / blood pressure
good
Low-fat diet/low chol.

Family
Rarely finds time to attend
child's special events
Too busy to spend much
time with family

Family
Attend most of child's
events
Makes time for family
regularly

Professional
Computer illiterate
Ineffective people skills

Professional
Efficient computer user
Strong people skills

Educational
One basic economics course

Educational
Bachelors degree

Spiritual
Inactive church-goer
No involvement with
church family

Spiritual
Active church-goer
Member of a church
family

This exercise presents a tiny sample for a model of how you would assemble your two sets of identities. If you have a significant difference between the two, set goals of growing from who you are now to whom you desire to be.

Merge Your Identities

The key goal is working to align your current and desired identities toward harmony. Craft the person you desire to be with the person you are now. Make the character of that new, best person the *real you*. When you do, you will feel comfortable with the perceived identity of you by others.

Strong people (strong in the right ways) waste little time worrying about how they are perceived by others.

Being focused on helping others and creating value, they are too emotionally secure to worry about their image. However, if someone is intentionally trying to distort your identity for their gain at your expense, you must challenge them immediately. Then, let the truth expose itself.

In every human being, there is naturally some distance and conflict between these two identities because no one is a perfect reflection of their highest desires.

If you have severe conflict between your current and desired identities, you are incurring a lot of stress because you are most likely violating your value system. You may also be falling short of your desires, dreams, and goals. It has been said that, "Who you actually are, compared to whom you desire to be, equals your self-esteem."

How can you close the gap between your current and desired identities? Read on and we'll discuss merging your identities by:

- Establishing empowering beliefs.
- Aligning a value system that is a reflection of those beliefs.

- Setting goals that provide specific destinations and plans for your life.

SalesMinds clarify their purposes, improve their self-esteem, and gain confidence by knowing who they are now and who they desire to become.

BELIEFS AND PURPOSE

I believe... Beliefs are the psychological foundation of purpose. All other thoughts, emotions, and actions spring from the things you believe. Your beliefs define you. They motivate you. They enable you to persist when times are tough. They are the basis on which you take action (more in Chapter 3, Action). If everything and everyone were taken away from you in a flash, you would be left alone with your core beliefs.

Define and intensify the beliefs that support your mission. As you do this, dismantle the beliefs that attack your mission. Remember, your daily mindset rests on the foundation of the things you believe. Some beliefs empower and generate greatness. Some beliefs drain people and may ultimately destroy them. Take out your journal and write down some key beliefs you truthfully possess:

- **I possess these type of positive and supportive beliefs that I need to strengthen:**

I believe that sales success is a combination of attitude, skill, product knowledge development, and a solid spiritual foundation.

I believe that a constant thirst for growth, and lifelong habits of learning, are crucial to success in life.

Yours:

Now, on a separate journal page, write down any negative beliefs you might have. Here are two samples of destructive beliefs you *could* possess:

- **I possess these type of negative destructive beliefs that I need to abandon:**

It's unfair for some people to have more money than others who work just as hard.

Since great salespeople are born, not made, I'll never be one because I wasn't born with the gift of gab.

Yours:

The purpose of a well-defined belief system is to create a solid launching pad from which appropriate desires can effectively operate.

VALUES AND PURPOSE

I value... What is important to you at all times? It's what you value. The Bible says, "Where your heart is, there also is your treasure." Do you realize that what you place value on (through your actions) should be a direct reflection of what you believe in? The proper description of the relationship between a belief and a value is, "I believe, *therefore* I value." But, being human, what we value through our actions may be inconsistent with what we believe or what we say we believe. If you claim to believe in charity, you should therefore value contributing. But if you never give a dime, is your belief in line with your value? Of course not.

A value is defined as "a principle, standard, or quality considered inherently worthwhile or desirable." I was once told that you can tell a person's values by looking at their daily planner and checkbook, that is, at how they spend their *time* and *money*. Values are the important priorities of life and business. A value system is best manifested as a written-out set of priorities that constitute the person's core. It defines their reasons for living, their motives for persisting, and their absolute foundations of certainty for their life. They are absolutely necessary when times get tough or schedules get hectic. A person should define the platform of what they value as if it were placed upon the pillars of their belief system. Those definitions are a value system. Do you have a value system that is congruent with your beliefs? Is it in writing?

Why does a person need a value system? Because everyone has the need for attachment to a foundation when they make the big and little decisions of everyday life. They need well-defined, ethical, and worthwhile motivators that attach importance to the sacrifices and energies of their lives. When you marry a defined value with desire, you will have powerful offspring!

A value system also serves the role of an instant signaling system when your thoughts or actions are moving in the opposite direction of your values. Values also establish courage to respond when you are challenged by another person or group. Others can influence you in a manner that would violate your value system. Stand up for what's really important, and don't compromise your values!

Is a Proper Value System Relative?

Does one person's value system (even if well-defined) have the same moral and ethical worth as any other person's? No. Relativity means that one person's value system (based on their own lifestyle, thoughts, beliefs, and circumstances) would have the same validity as any other person's. That's not necessarily the case, I would argue.

What if one person values violence, disruption, and lawlessness, while another person values peace, order, and legal authority? I believe a person must establish a value system (with some moral absolutes) based on the following priorities:

1. **Spiritual:** My personal values would ask, what does the Bible say about any given issue as a value standard?

2. **Ethical:** Are my values right, honest, and truthful?

3. **Contributing:** Do my values contribute to someone else's welfare and growth?

4. **Enriching:** Does the pursuit of my values invest in myself and others, or does it only represent consumption with no added benefit?

I stand on the position that any individual determination of value (what is right and important to pursue) has a standard of construction and is not an arbitrary assessment based on any array of lifestyles, feelings, and circumstances (relativity).

I'm not alone. The Princeton Research Center reports that 64 percent of Americans are dissatisfied with ethics and morals in our society. Furthermore, 73 percent are dissatisfied with the level of honesty and standards. In this new age, you can still believe in some old ideas. Values without morals are useless.

Create Your Own Value System Now

I challenge you to invest some time now with a legal pad to clarify a set of proper values for your life in writing. I did this many years ago, and it has been one of the strongest anchors I have ever established in my life for my goals and decisions:

Step One: On your pad, brainstorm in writing 12 – 15 categories in general terms of what you consider to be important in life on a sheet of paper. Don't worry about getting the words right, getting them in order, or the surface emotional reactions you'll have. Just define the areas, people, and focal points of what is most important to you in life. Get it down. Ask yourself:

- Would I be happy if everything else were stripped away but these values?
- How can I put my values into specific words?
- Where did I get my values?
- Are my values really my own?
- Are my values someone else's (like my parents) but not necessarily mine?
- If my life took a quick turn, would I still value them?
- If I got rich now, would I still value them?

Another key consideration for your values: Do any of them (be honest) have a destructive downside? That means if you act out a value (for example, freedom within a relationship) will it be harmful to you or others? It's not hard to find people who had values that destroyed them. Consider Bonnie and Clyde, Jimi Hendrix, and Timothy McVay. And don't forget the business fates and troubles of Martha Stewart; Michael Milliken; Ivan Boske; Enron Corp's Ken Lay, Ben Glisan Jr., and Dan Boyle; and various executives of WorldCom and Global Crossing.

Step Two: Force yourself to rank those general value categories 1 – 10, with 1 as most important. Do this on a separate piece of paper. Key for ranking: If value #3 were taken away overnight, would you still stand strong and still desire values #1 and #2? Why?

Step Three: Develop sub-hierarchies within your categories. For example, within "family": First, wife and kids. Second, parents. Third, brothers and sisters. Fourth, extended family and so on. Again, why?

Step Four: Work on the word precision and sequence of your value statements.

Step Five: Step back and finally ask: Is all this true? If your written value system is now defined truthfully, congratulations! Type it up and keep it with you because it is one of the most important assets you will ever possess.

SalesMinds gain purpose by aligning what they desire with what they know is truly valuable.

GOALS AND PURPOSE

I want... How do you specifically define your important desired achievements? You do so by combining your identities, beliefs, and values into a written blueprint for achievement. All of your thoughts can then be crystallized and put into action. These are the focused plans of desire; they are your goals.

Use the following goal model to shape and reinforce your desires. (Rule #1, the goals have to be yours, not someone else's. Many people set themselves up for failure by trying to meet the expectations of another's goal). Goals should be in a framework, operate like a roadmap, and should be:

- Written
- Balanced between short and long term directions
- Prioritized
- Believable
- Mutually-generated with a spouse or boss (if applicable)
- Detailed
- Centralized in one notebook or planner
- Updated and reviewed
- Exciting (boring goals get boring results)
- Sustainable
- Measurable (have a deadline)
- Balanced in life areas
- Resource considerate
- Defined as material or non-material
- Flexible to certain changes
- Considerate of resistance
- Defined with a starting point
- Aware of any relevant conditions
- Computerized or otherwise electronically assisted (accessible on a PDA, for example)

Key for making your goals more vivid and emotional: Besides just words, use every available focus (tool) like mental images, photos, diagrams, and descriptions to stimulate the senses to help define these desires. Construct your goals using vivid imagination as if you had *already* achieved them.

*Sales*Minds *gain purpose by defining their specific goals in writing.*

Purpose is the *motive* of desire. But alone, even the most worthy desires will never lead to success. There is another key ingredient in activating your purpose into reality. It is the success clue left behind by all high achievers, and one that is clearly evident in the following experience I'll never forget.

ACTION

DO IT NOW

S haring stories about my early days at Lanier selling copiers is something I don't do much anymore. At about twenty calls a day and countless sales as a rep and manager, there are just too many to talk about. But I'll always remember this one.

Starting on the early morning of the last Friday in November of 1983, I had nine sales on the board and needed three more that day to claim Lanier's newest and most prestigious monthly award called, "The Dirty Dozen," which carried a $1500.00 bonus.

I wanted this achievement badly and decided that this day would be the most action-rich sales day of my career. My problem: most of what could be closed—I had exhausted about everything nearby—was about seventy miles away from the office in the farthest corners of my territory. Not to mention another problem: selling copiers is fundamentally hard. My tactics for the day follow:

First I planned my day. I considered the possible sales, their locations, the highways, and my available time, and marked out my most efficient route on the map.

Then I warmed up with six or eight cold calls before heading out to my targets, having collected nothing but rejection. Three sales were still a must.

I found one. At about 11 a.m. on about my fifteenth cold call in the most distant corner of the territory, at Rockmart, Georgia, I discovered a small funeral home that didn't even have a copier. The director was happy to see me; we went through several demonstrations of copiers I brought in from my van, and he bought one about 1:00 p.m. I thanked him and jumped in the van because I still needed two more sales. Time was short.

(Nineteen years later, I attended a memorial service at this same home, Alvis Miller & Son. Amazingly, the director, Melton Moss, was still there and remembered me! He also said he had been very pleased with his purchase, the immediate delivery and installation, and the fair price for his needs.)

Knowing I was too far out, I looked at the cards of every possible buyer I had previously talked to. I decided to cut a straight path to several businesses I had already shown copiers to before. There simply wasn't time to convert purely cold calls into the two sales I had to have.

I had only one small, reconditioned copier left onboard, so I called back on a used car dealer (really) in Dallas, Georgia. The copier I had was perfect for his small volume of copies for titles and sales contracts. *He bought it* on the spot by putting $500.00 cash on the platen of the copier, and signed the receipt. I installed it and headed out. It was about 5:00 and still one short of twelve. In addition, final orders at the office were supposed to be in no later than 5:30 p.m. to close out the month.

I was on a level of adrenaline that told me loud and clear, "You've got to do it." I pulled out about four remaining 3 x 5 cards with notes for the only remaining possible sales between where I was and the office.

I would have just one more stab at making an effective call to score one more sale. A small restaurant where I had made a number of calls and demonstrations over the previous six months with no luck was in a direct line to the office. I bolted for it, knowing the owner would have to be there for this to become a decision. On the drive I mentally planned every necessary action to make it happen.

They were just coming on shift for the dinner business when I arrived and the owner was there. I don't even remember how we greeted and why he agreed to carve out a few minutes of time (when buying the copier right then was probably the last thing on his mind). Perhaps he saw something in my eyes that inspired him to respond.

Finally, *I got an order from him* for a copier on a lease agreement that really could be of value to his restaurant with some supply incentives in return for a decision right then and there. I told him about The Dirty Dozen contest and that I had to get this order back to be processed immediately. He wanted to help me, I felt sure.

He assured me he had made a good business decision on the copier and its applications for him.

I got the order in late but it was credited, won the award, and got the bonus. Every ounce of energy I had that day was gone. I had left everything on the field and won the game. It was time to go home and get ready for the next month starting Monday. That's the way it was at Lanier.

About two weeks later, our regional manager came to visit our office and, as was normal, he huddled up with my district manager behind closed doors. I was just about to head out to the territory when my boss asked me to come in and talk to them both. Then came the shocker: After a bout with buyer's remorse, the owner of the restaurant of my twelfth sale decided he could actually do some of the functions intended for the copier another way. He wanted to void the sale and return the copier. They told me he felt bad but had to reverse his prior decision.

I was devastated. I assumed my bonus and the award would be stripped from me. They also told me the restaurant's owner, Fred Aiken, a state representative in the Georgia Legislature, was a close personal friend of our CEO and president, Wes Cantrell. I could feel the hot water boiling and was just speechless. How badly had I damaged my young career?

My bosses voided the sale and took the copier back. However, they were *impressed* with my sales efforts on the contest's final day and decided that this level of personal effort was the standard for the entire company. So they upheld my award and bonus.

Nine months later, on a Lanier award trip to the Bahamas, I was standing by the hotel pool talking to the other winners from around the country when Mr. Cantrell approached me. I swallowed nervously as we shook hands.

He told me that each year at the new-hire-school he addresses the troops for about fifteen minutes to welcome them to the company. He went on to say that one story he now tells them is how I won the Dirty Dozen award by selling his friend Fred at the eleventh hour, and that if they wanted to be the best at Lanier, *this is what they needed to do too.*

I've never been the same since.

Action is the DNA of achievement. You can sit around all you want thinking about success or you can gear up, go out, and do the work. It is the one element that you see in all achievement: taking results-getting actions.

Consider my Lanier story. That story is reality because I took a high degree of desire and backed it with action. No action, no award, no bonus (and no story).

ACTION IS THE EXECUTION OF DESIRE

Action is defined as "a thing done, behavior, conduct, or the process or fact of doing something." Notice the word "done." Enough "dones" will shape the destiny of an entire life.

A *Sales*Mind converts a clear purpose into action. Action is what converts intention into reality. Leveraging action will culminate into a position of real results; manifested desire feeds upon those results to achieve even more.

A *Sales*Mind thrives on action (not just intention). Intention is the desire to sell more. Action *creates* the sales.

To be a true success, action has to become a habit, a knee-jerk response.

Don't waste too much time worrying about how to do something, just do it! One of the most powerful and immediately noticeable attributes of *Sales*Minds is their habit of acting quickly to get the job done.

They're taking action, making the tough calls, getting the correspondence out, setting closing appointments with real decision-makers, and reaping benefits when the herd is sitting around still planning and strategizing. Procrastination is the enemy of the *Sales*Mind, who is committed to taking urgent action. As you plan for rapid, effective action, consider these issues:

- **Knowledge:** Do you know what to do?
- **Speed:** Do you act quickly on a plan?
- **Motive:** Do you act with the right intentions?
- **Character:** Do you do what you say?

However, the key issue is: Are you a *doer* or an *intender*? Your future success depends on what actions you take to prove that you're a doer. The many disappointments of mediocrity follow when you don't take action, thus proving that you're merely an intender.

From Now Until Death?

The first line of a book I once read was IGDS, an acronym for "I'm Going to Die Someday." And you will. Me too. The point is that from now until that day, we only have a limited amount of time to achieve, and to achieve it takes action. That's a sobering perspective.

Recently a close friend wrote to tell me about an apparently healthy, vibrant, and successful young woman who had unexpectedly died at 38 of a brain aneurysm. This young lady was old in terms of her total life and she didn't realize it.

It has been said that a person is only considered old when their regrets take the place of their dreams. Take action now to move toward your dreams and joys, and banish all memory of your regrets and pains. Whichever plan you choose to pursue will be your constant companion later in life.

"Faith by itself, if it is not accompanied by deeds, is dead."
——James 2:17

Action Challenges

Taking action has many roadblocks. It is acceptable to consider and deal with the challenges of taking action. It is *unacceptable* to be either ignorant of them or to use these challenges as excuses not to act:

- Lack of focus and purpose.
- Lack of money or resources.
- Lack of time.
- Lack of energy.
- Laziness.
- Apathy.
- Poor upbringing or past environment.
- Poor present environment.
- A belief that someone else (like the government) will take action to take care of you.
- A lack of accessible knowledge.

- Ineffective emotional management.
- No goals or plans.
- Sustaining a setback.
- Sustaining a disaster.
- Improper evaluation and adjustment of previous actions that failed.

I have a belief. If for one day, a person could be allowed to forget all the reasons they shouldn't do something, and just do it without contemplation, their results would soar.

*Sales***Minds** *understand that action is the vehicle to convert desire into results.*

THE EFFECTS OF ACTION

The "Inverse Effect": Do What You Don't Like

The things you like to do often are not productive, and many of the things you don't like to do often are extremely productive. This is a key dimension of successful people. To get results, they make themselves do the things they don't like to do. It's also called self-discipline.

Not long ago I saw a short TV interview of a man named John Paul DeJoria, the co-founder of the highly successful Paul Mitchell line of hair care products you see in salons. He was asked by the interviewer, "What is one thing you could tell us that attributed to your success?" His answer: "I learned when we started in 1979 to do the hard things other people didn't like to do, and those things made us successful." That's the inverse effect of taking action.

The Greatest Effects of Action are Cumulative and Unknown

Action reveals the (unknown) door of opportunity. The most powerful results of action come not from what we know will happen, but rather from what we don't know will happen. I call that the "cumulative effect," rather than the immediate effect, of action. Americans are very conditioned to the immediate effect of action, or getting immediate returns for what we do. We have microwaves for quick food, we go down to the convenience store, and we shop online. We also become frustrated when we don't get an immediate result from our invested time and energy. But, as a *Sales*Mind, you can't afford to believe that all your sales calls and actions will return direct results. Some of your actions will return results you don't expect and create unforeseen opportunities.

To illustrate the cumulative (and unknown) effect of action, you might get two or three good responses from a personal mailer if you mailed 100. But you wouldn't know which ones (prior to mailing) would respond. That's an unknown outcome that was based on the faith in the law of percentages of that mailer. So until you mailed the 100, which two or three would you have called?

A *Sales*Mind simply has faith that consistent action will create a percentage of good results. The Bible says *we reap what we sow*—an easy law to forget. What about your cumulative actions? Can you count on results? Yes. You can believe that your actions will create opportunity. And when it knocks, answer the door and seize it!

Predicting Effective Action

It is vital to know categorically *which* types of actions produce results. A *Sales*Mind will be able to predict effective action through the awareness that:

- Every action will produce some result, even if that result is rejection. According to a primary law of physics, "Every action has an equal and opposite reaction."
- Actions proven to produce positive results by you in the past will produce positive results again.
- Actions proven to produce positive results by others may produce similar positive results if taken by you.

*Sales***Minds** *desire to take difficult actions, and possess the knowledge and confidence to know that those actions will pay off.*

WHAT ARE THE MOTIVES OF ACTION?

The short answer: The things just defined that have purpose. Focus, purpose, and action need to interconnect for a *Sales*Mind. Otherwise, you're in a state of conflict or indecision. Selling is a time/energy allocation business on the part of the seller. With this in mind, there are three key motives that work hand-in-hand to act out a strong sense of purpose:

- Specific personal, positive beliefs about business.
- The desire to maximize the effectiveness of action within limited time.
- Fear of the consequences of not taking action.

Let's examine each of these motives.

Action Follows Belief

To believe is to "accept as true or real, to have confidence, to trust, to expect, or to suppose." Positive belief also triggers productive, effective action. And while purpose initiates action, belief sustains it. You will *act on* what you strongly *believe in*.

Develop a personal mission statement or diary in writing that strengthens these five beliefs:

1. **I believe in myself.**
2. **I believe that focusing on service and value** for my buyers creates the by-product of income for me, not vice versa.
3. **I believe in my company and its products,** and that they deliver those elements of value. If I lack this belief, I need to work somewhere else.
4. **I believe wholeheartedly in the daily business of selling,** which is the transfer of value to the buyer in exchange for money.
5. **I believe that I deserve selling's best returns.**

What You Could Have Been—If You Had More Time

The past is gone and the future is yet to occur. Therefore, a *Sales*Mind has to have a sense of urgency to execute priorities *today*. But, when is taking action appropriate, most effective, and most necessary? The answer almost always is NOW. This very moment, this fleeting instant called "now," is the only exact moment over which you have control, or will ever have control. A *Sales*Mind develops a personal sense of urgency to act in two consistent ways:

Initial Action. This is the habit of taking a first small action step immediately toward an objective without hesitation or procrastination. The initial actions might be the first steps in a process: the copy for the key contact letter, the first of a series of phone calls to get through to a key person, the first contact early in the morning, or the first action toward an important goal. A *Sales*Mind knows that initial, even unplanned action, creates the forward momentum that success in sales demands.

Sales power multiplies when a little bit of focused action is applied to develop the momentum to get through a project successfully. Substitute your worry time with action time. Set up your systems, tools, habits, and times to invite first-step, low-intensity action to build momentum. Think of your first actions as those of an athlete stretching to warm-up before competition.

Sustaining Action. Do you have the habit of taking the continuous actions in a sales cycle or project to see it through to decision or outcome? These are the actions of *persistence*. Sustaining actions are for the next contact, the next appointment, or goals for the next quarter. It's not enough to start a process. You have to be a strong finisher.

Be Afraid of Not Taking Action

> *"The fear of failure is so great with me I want to avoid that miserable four days after a loss by doing anything I can do."*
> —— **Curt Schilling**
> Arizona Diamondback's all-star pitcher

Psychologists have determined that the perceived pain of loss is three times greater than the perceived joy of gain. That reality can be an influence to compel a *Sales*Mind to take action to achieve success because they have an intense fear of being unsuccessful. In this case, fear isn't bad because it heightens your senses and intensifies your focus.

SalesMinds *desire to take action because their time and beliefs are precious. This desire exists along with a motivating fear of not taking action.*

ACTION ALLOCATION

A *Sales*Mind also knows how to engineer their actions and time planning so as to achieve the best possible position in their business. In chapter 9, Priority, we will define how to determine the most important buyers and activities for our actions. But in general, a *Sales*Mind takes five kinds of sales actions every day:

1. Actions that prepare for contact with someone.
2. Actions of physical or phone contact.
3. Actions of follow-up after a contact.
4. Actions with buyers to expand account relationships or render service.
5. Actions that are internal to the company or that educate.

This perspective on the allocation of action is crucial to growing a sales territory or account base. Action is only productive in the sales business when it is action of the right kind. To help allocate our specific sales actions, we should be aware of which actions are best in terms of productivity and which actions are ineffective.

Here is a 3-category list to help you classify the effectiveness of your actions:

1. **BEST SALES ACTIONS:**
    Appointment or activity with a decision-maker
    Serving a buyer
    Presentation to a new prospect
    Consistent coverage
    Educating buyers to expand the relationship
    Telephone activity
    Moving a sale forward

    Percent of your day?_____

2. **SECONDARY ACTIONS**
    Strategy or planning
    Setting a goal

Evaluation or analysis
Creating new sales ideas
Data input
Effective internal meetings or training
Time planning

Percent of your day?_____

3. **INEFFECTIVE ACTIONS**
Wishing for something
Unnecessary meetings
Worrying
Doing paperwork during selling hours
Associating with negative people
Doing work twice
Poor or short work habits

Percent of your day?_____

For your specific buyers, exactly what type of action will have the strongest and best impact at this particular moment? A letter? A phone call? A gift? A fax? An email? A meeting? This approach is called a "contact mix," and we will detail this mix in Chapter 11, Coverage.

Sales*Minds *allocate their actions to accomplish their desires.

FOLLOW UP WITH MORE ACTION

Do you plan with forethought your next action of follow-up with a buyer? Buyers cool off after interaction with you, so you need to apply productive follow-up techniques to reopen a sales conversation and move toward your key request, which is to elicit a buying commitment of some nature.

Some buyers you have known for years may also take more of your energy and action before they make a purchase. That's OK. Just factor in that knowledge without feeling frustrated. If you do, they will buy again and again.

These follow-up techniques produce results:

1. **Call back** and extend a planned offer, free gift, beneficial new idea, or information update.
2. **Call back** with a specific request for information that will open up more discussion toward the sale.
3. **Call back** and share a comment from another person in the buyer's company about how positive your presentation was received by their department.

All of those "re-openers" are effective ways to get you and the buyer back on the value-focus of your program.

Successful selling demands taking one desired action after another after another after another...

PULL YOURSELF OUT OF A SLUMP WITH ACTION

A slump in the sales business is a defeated emotional state that has the *by-product* of low sales. If you don't think it is mostly emotional, look at the sales results that often occur when you replace an emotionally defeated salesperson with an energetic, hungry, and excited new sales rep itching for an opportunity. High activity (along with strong faith) is the best security to climb quickly out of a slump and to never have one again. A *Sales*Mind must focus on these actions if ever in a slump:

1. **Eliminate or diminish** the emotional impact of negative thought (See Chapter 1, Focus).
2. **Distance yourself** from negative people and avoid talking to them as much as you can because you'll always come away from them feeling deflated.
3. **Initiate a new campaign** of specific prospecting activity every week and measure its effectiveness.
4. **Go for simple wins.**
5. **Read and pray.**
6. **Interact** with lots of positive people.
7. **Focus on one sale only** for now to gain momentum.
8. **After that sale,** give yourself a special reward; such as a dinner or a special movie.
9. **Recommit and rewrite** why and how you can help buyers with your program.

Climbing out of a slump isn't planning for down the road. It is changing the slump condition immediately. Your ability to *plan* the future is never as valuable as your ability to *determine* your future with action right now.

*Rekindling desire into action is the locomotive that will pull a Sales*Mind *out of a rare slump.*

Action is the *execution* of desire. It creates success momentum. But every success endeavor is tested with challenges, objections, and obstacles. So now it's important to examine the next level of skills that were launched with an action but have evolved into a need for reaction.

4

RESPONSE

IT'S HOW YOU REACT

W hen my father died of a sudden heart attack at 72, it devastated our family. He was a beloved family man, Christian, husband of forty-seven years, and a role model of the highest degree. He was here one moment, active and vibrant, and gone in a flash. You never get over this type of loss when you deeply love someone. But you are forced to *respond* to it.

You struggle with "why" and "what if" and "I should have." You are hammered with the impact of what happened. You suffer from a new resistance created by the daily pain of being forced to carry on without him.

In time, when the major shock subsided, I made a decision based on an answer to this simple question, "How would Dad want me to respond?" My decision was that I would, to the best of my ability, take my pain of loss and convert it into positive energy.

My response to Dad's death was to focus even more energy on my contributions to my own family and those I influence. That is without question what he would have wanted. His death became a cause. I was committed to making my response to his absence a source of personal strength—an addition to my life, not a subtraction.

What about the circumstances and pressures *you* are (or have been) faced with in life and business? Are you responding to them in the best ways possible? Are those pressures creating deterioration in your life, or growth and maturity?

RESPONSE IS THE TEST OF DESIRE

"Let's Roll."
—— **President George W. Bush**

To honor him, the president was quoting Todd Beamer, one of the American heroes of 9/11 who helped divert hijacked Flight 93 to an empty Pennsylvania field instead of into our crowded capital city.

Response is defined as "a reaction to a specific stimulus." A stimulus is the generator of your attention: a sudden experience, a sight, a sound, an emotion, a problem, an issue, an objection, a conversation, or an opportunity.

From the moment you exited the womb and the doctor spanked your little bottom, you discovered that stimuli and responses are inherent to independent life.

But as a *Sales*Mind, do you have to respond to everything pressing for your attention? No. You can't respond to every person, problem, question, condition, or political issue. Sometimes, it is wise to let time alone provide the outcome. You do nothing. Your neutral response allows time to work out the solution, which will often be a better outcome for you than unnecessarily committing yourself.

The danger in selling is that your hesitation and "wisdom" may really be lack of skill, poor preparation, or simple procrastination—the most deadly reason of all. None of those negative excuses for inaction—and a host of other similar ones—are wise when you have constant deadlines for performing. A *Sales*Mind responds with thoughts, words, and actions to get command of these issues:

- **Pressure**: Selling is always a pressure-cooker to meet quotas each month. Therefore, the consistent quantity, speed, and quality of your responses are crucial to compress results within that month. For example, if within thirty days it takes one hundred various responses to generate ten sales, and you respond only thirty times, you'll get only about three sales, never ten.

- **Passivity**: Can you afford the luxury of waiting for most sales goals and issues to work out without responding? *Sales*Minds don't wait. They know that if they neglect, suppress, or somehow avoid responding to opportunities, a faster, more aggressive competitor will snatch the prize from under their noses.

- **Precision**: A *Sales*Mind has responses to life and business that are selective and skilled. That's why they study, practice, and train. When a *Sales*Mind responds, it is with strong, balanced skills that are conditioned to the point of being a reflex. The reflex comes from successful action under pressure.

Adhering to these tough-minded rules develops character. Just look at the lives of people you admire and examine how they deal, or dealt, with their pressures. They achieved their positive results by responding to them.

How you respond to what happens is far more important than what actually happens. A SalesMind understands this vital truth.

RESPOND TO RESISTANCE

Sales and business stimuli generate two basic conditions, *opportunity* and *resistance*:

Opportunity is the grease that moves you forward. *Sales*Minds develop the timing, knowledge, and discernment that enable them to respond to opportunities. Those stimuli might be another's smile, a buying signal, new market data, a referral, or body language. Most of this book is devoted to seizing opportunity, so we'll devote most of our time in this chapter to responding to resistance.

Resistance is the friction that slows you down. To *Sales*Minds, the common forms of resistance to sales in general and to sales in their field are *known* and can be *anticipated*. These are things such as people guarding their money, or their lack of desire to change suppliers.

Other resistances are *unknown* and can either creep up or hit you out of the blue. For example, a decision-maker unknown to you is blocking your proposal's approval. A *Sales*Mind accepts the constant reality of resistance in causing business-like setbacks, delays, frustrations, disappointments, deferrals, objections, lack of response, competition, price pressure, or difficulty in getting a new buyer's attention. These items of resistance simply provide a platform to establish many effective positive responses.

Resistance to a *Sales*Mind is an opportunity to respond. Either act now (which also strengthens you) or ignore the issue and move on to another one.

> *"I delight in weakness, in insults, in hardships, in*
> *persecutions, in difficulties.*
> *For when I am weak, then I am strong."*
> —— **Galatians 12:10**

*A **Sales**Mind knows that resistance will either destroy or fuel desire.*

RESPOND WITH DESIRE

Opportunity and resistance always come into contact with these levels of your desire to achieve:

- When your high level of desire meets or creates opportunity, you will flourish as a person. That's power *harmony*.

- When your lack of desire meets high resistance, you will pull back and recede from the potential buyer's view. That's retreat—but not necessarily defeat.

All highly skilled people understand how to leverage these relationships. What about you? Are you basically moving forward or backward in your sales life? Do you know how to regain forward leverage if you need it?

Personal Response Principles

- Your desire to maximize opportunity must be substantially greater than the resistance you face to achieve. This positive relationship moves you forward toward your goals. That is why it is critical to be focused on goals that have purpose and to support your purpose with decisive action.

- Your life will move alternately forward and backward at various times. You will always experience some combination of setbacks and breakthroughs. So you must have a faster and more decisive movement forward than backward to gain ground.

- Your forward motion and achievement occur when you respond to stimuli (pressures, problems, and objections) with skill and decisive action. That will enable your desires to dominate.

- When you don't respond skillfully or at all, the resistance gains momentum, becomes the dominant force, and now you are moving backward.

- For you to be effective, your desire and resistance cannot be equal. Your desire must be substantially greater than your resistance, or resistance will win by wearing you down emotionally. Pain gets an edge on gain and commands your attention.

  For example, let's say your *desire* is producing a level of sales income averaging $10,000 per month, and your *resistance* of bills and taxes is $9800. That is a very tight break-even level. You can easily start falling behind because your setbacks outpace your achievements for a short time.

  This observation is not negative; it's just practical. The grind of bills every month never fails; the leads for revenue are not always as dependable.

  Keep desires ahead of resistance with as wide a margin as possible. Plan to build disposable income, not simply income to meet bills already incurred.

- Your responses have financial value: If sales success were easy for your company, they would hire minimum wage workers to fill orders. Handling resistance in sales is the basis of your value and the most compelling reason why you are paid to represent a company. I call this skill "response-ability." It is therefore economically justifiable for your company to expect you to respond to buyer pressures, expectations, and internal company demands.

• Your "resistance persistence" is your insurance policy to win: Winners try, then fall down, yet get up and try again. Responding may not always be a first action to an objection or problem, but might be a secondary or follow-up action. Your series of buyer responses may take months or years to win a victory, so keep on responding *relentlessly*. Use a variety of responses, but keep on responding and responding. Be like the Energizer® bunny that "just keeps going and going and going—"

> *"Failure cannot cope with persistence."*
> —— **Napoleon Hill**

• Your specific resistances and desires need to square off: What is your specific relationship of these two emotional dimensions in your life? Which dimension strikes with the heaviest impact? Start with a few of those listed on the next page, and then make your own lists by tailoring them to your unique circumstances:

RESISTANCES   VS.   DESIRES

Fear	Faith
Money pressure	Financial success
Short-sightedness	Vision
Seller greed	Compulsion to serve
Seller indifference	Seller conviction
Feature-focus	Value-focus
Uncertainty	Goals and direction
Fearful of the future	Realizing potential
Family obligations	Having and giving love
Lack of time	Maximizing opportunities
Poor health	High energy and vitality
Fearful of criticism	Capable and confident

Do any of these resistances and desires fit you? It's like a financial balance sheet: Your desire net worth shows you either owe (resistances) more than you own (desires) or vice versa.

For your desires to move forward, the grease of opportunity must overpower the friction of resistance.

RESPOND TO FEAR

Resistance's driving force is the emotion of *fear*. Fear is anticipated pain, mostly unrealized. Fear chokes people. It chokes their character and their dreams. It turns them into victims instead of victors. Dealing with fear is always a factor in response effectiveness. We often have hesitation or fear in our reaction because we are:

- Unaware of how critical our response skills are.
- Lazy or unfocused.
- Afraid of criticism or embarrassment.
- Intimidated by the circumstance or a person.
- Ill-trained in skill.
- Unaccustomed to reacting quickly.
- Lacking information to respond appropriately.
- Hesitant to be branded as a high-pressure sales person.
- Hoping if we do nothing the problem will go away.

Unfortunately, any of these fear elements, if they take root, will plunge you in the opposite direction of being effective and productive. Worse yet, you may lose self-esteem and confidence, both of which can cause your defeat as a salesperson.

Do Something

Fear has to be dealt with and minimized to leverage desire. A *Sales*Mind responds to fear with awareness, action, and repetition. Responding also requires faith and self-confidence. Go back to the Action chapter you just read and put it into play.

Your needed action may be a tough sales appointment, a verbal response, or a physical movement. Take action today and respond to your challenges. Many of them are opportunities.

You'll be glad you responded, immediately for what you achieve, and lastingly for what you will see demon-strated: the superiority of action over inaction. Equally important, taking action now means you may have regained forward motion if you lost it.

Whatever your circumstance—do something!

Overcoming hesitation and fear with timely, confident responses is vital in maintaining desire.

RESPOND IN ALL DIMENSIONS

You may meet with a combination of resistances, all happening *at the same time*. This calls for a multi-dimensional response. Everyone has various levels of pressure and resistance, all occurring daily in different ways and intensities. Most of these pressures require responses. *Sales*Minds must:

1. **Respond to the overall constant pressures in life to succeed.** Resistance can come from competition, the market, friends, family, the achievement of wealth, weakness of certain vital skills, geography, difficult accumulated emotions, and more. These generalized conditions of life today in our culture spawn the emotions of fear, helplessness, hopelessness, hesitation, reluctance, frustration, and disappointment. Every human being faces degrees of overall resistance. We have massive amounts in our society because of the demands of our higher lifestyle standards.

2.   **Respond to personal adversity.** Adversities are those traumatic, devastating, and highly emotional circumstances that can happen in anyone's life, such as the death of a loved one, rejection, financial hardship, disappointment, and so on. Adversity is a platform from which you have to rebound and go on. Life and business will continue with or without you. Effective response to adversity develops intense resilience. Intense resilience converts negative past energy into the current positive energy needed to produce results. You must firmly establish the belief in your mind that every setback carries with it the seed of a greater benefit.

3.   **Respond to buyer resistance.** *Sales*Minds ask buyers to exchange their money for superior product and service value. When a buyer is not responding, a *Sales*Mind must determine the cause, determine whether to respond, or move on to another buyer. The basic reasons buyers do not respond to sales approaches are:

- No attention offered to the seller.
- No need for the product or service.
- No urgency to change.
- No money available.
- No trust in the seller.
- Not enough perceived value for the money (your price).
- Not as high a level of perceived value for the money as from a your competitor (your competitor's lower price).

- No problem has surfaced or they are not sufficiently disturbed about an existing problem.

As part of success in sales, every *Sales*Mind will have some combination of these dimensions of resistance. They will come in various shapes, sizes, and magnitudes, but all should evoke an appropriate response from you.

For these resistances, *Sales*Minds create and rehearse exact, conditioned verbal and physical responses, drilling themselves on their responses until they become natural reflexes. There arc no shortcuts. If you can't respond by reflex, you don't stand a chance in reaching your potential.

Sales*Minds *respond to pressures of various types and magnitudes, intensifying their desire in the process.

RESPOND WITH POWERFUL MINDSETS

Just as fear has to be dealt with, a *Sales*Mind also has to create the proper *mindsets* for handling resistance. These attitudes are the basis for your actions and responses. When negative mental resistance enters any of these mindsets, it is swallowed up and minimized. Program into your mind right now these mindsets, one by one, so you can access them at will. Say to yourself: "I choose to operate with the following attitudes:"

- **Faith**. I believe that God has a plan for me and that I am capable of great things, no matter what the resistance.

- **Choice**. I can either focus on the blame and unfairness of what happens to me (choose to be a victim) or respond to life and move on (choose to be a victor).

- **Acceptance**. Much that I can't control happens. A buyer might have a better friend than me to buy from, or my reputation may be new in this market area. This is the playing field of selling. There is nothing fair about sales. Deal with it; keep moving ahead.

- **Perspective**. What size is this resistance in relative terms to my personal or sales life? Take the perspective of income in America: The Heritage Foundation reports that a person in the bottom 10% of income in America still earns more than two-thirds of the people living in the rest of the world.

- **Frustration**. Any frustration I can't shrug off I neutralize with my mindset. I have frustration daily, and if not handled properly, it will overwhelm my efforts. Conquering this condition is the price of sales success.

- **Risk**. I have to say and do certain out-of-the-ordinary things in order to achieve results.

- **Replacement**. I am confident that I can contribute value, find new business, and not be limited or satisfied with just my current buyers.

- **Calculation**. I am a financial seller. When it comes down to it, selling is dealing with money. Always on paper, I sell every value difference, percentage, ratio, comparison, depreciation, extension, amortization, and reduction in numbers, fluidly and calmly. A sales transaction involves money, and money is best represented in visual mathematics.

A response mindset is the mental boxing ring a *Sales*Mind *establishes to battle resistance without disrupting desire.*

RESPOND WITH WORDS

*"**Sincerity**. Use no hurtful deceit. Think innocently and justly; and if you speak, speak accordingly."*
—— **Benjamin Franklin**
Number 7 of his "13 Virtues"

Every buyer on earth says, "Your price is too high." It's always "too high." They say that even if they don't mean it. Often it's a reflex, conditioned in a buyer from thousands of purchases made over many years. Sometimes it's a smokescreen for not having the money, or perhaps it masks another issue.

Here is the question: Is the buyer's reflexive "Your price is too high" quicker than your reflex to explain your value?

In the following dialogue, the buyer is the **stimulus** and you are the **response**:

Stimulus: "Your price is too high."
Response: "Let me ask you, in relation to what other price?"

Stimulus: "Compared to other proposals."
Response: "That's fine. Roughly, what's the difference?"

Stimulus: "About ten percent."
Response: "OK, so the question is, why would you invest an extra ten percent to go with us. Is that correct?

Stimulus: "Yes, that's the issue."
Response: "All right. Let's go back over the extra value we discussed and see if it's worth the ten percent."

A *Sales*Mind who can smoothly produce this kind of conditioned, verbal response at any time simply makes more money than another salesperson who fumbles the lines. Why? Because you handle verbal buyer resistance right then and there in a buyer interchange, and keep the sale moving. What's your option? To call back when they have cooled off? How much more time and effort does that take? A lot. The best time to persuade is when the buyers are hot, not later when they have cooled off.

You have to desire to possess verbal response skills. You must also believe in your responses, and they must be truthful. These skills are incredibly valuable. Begin the process of acquiring them today:

- Identify and collect sales objections in writing, one by one, for your industry.

- Use your sales team members to assist in that collection.
- Partner with your sales team members to brainstorm two intelligent, value-oriented verbal responses to each objection and write them down.
- Type up an orderly short document with your objections and responses.
- Practice in front of a mirror as many times as possible the responses when you hear those objections. I first did this when I was twenty-two years old, and it has been invaluable ever since.
- Record yourself on audio or video giving your responses. When you review you'll see what needs correction.
- Enlist your spouse or kids to read the objections out loud and critique your response. They will help because they want you to be more successful!
- Use the response ASAP in the field in a live situation. Command of a skill can never come outside of real life where the real money pressure is.
- Keep your list and practice the responses a few minutes each month. Add any new objections you may discover in the field.
- Get over the fear of responding verbally.
- Learn to sincerely listen and care for your buyer as you prepare to respond.

We always identify objections and define responses to them in writing at my live seminars. I get emails every month of incredible achievements from attendees who have become effective in handling objections. Verbal objections—whether given on the phone or in person—happen in a flash. Without this professional process, you will not develop this reflex. Don't expect it to just happen automatically with time and experience—because it won't.

The SalesMind standard for verbal skill is to be able to deliver the proper response under pressure, with sincerity, when money is on the line.

Response is the *test* of desire. And we have now covered the essence of blending your focus, purpose, actions, and responses together to sustain and fulfill your desires. It is only fitting that this desire formula would serve as a powerful force for driving the business of engaging and persuading buyers to transact with you. Next up: the money factor.

PART II: PERSUASION

LEVERAGING BUYERS

For over twenty years, I have sold, researched, and trained. I have also traveled, interviewed, and studied intensely this simple but profound question: What *really* makes a sale?

That question raises others: What are the pieces and the elements? What generates persuasion in a buyer?

All my studies have led me to the same conclusion: What really makes a sale is having a successful relationship with the buyer *based on what he or she values.*

To achieve that with multitudes of buyers—a vital goal for all *Sales*Minds—you must build a successful relationship position with the kind of decision-making buyers who generate transactions. To acquire that position, a buyer's perceived value of your program must out-leverage their perception of its price or their desire to obtain it somewhere else. In other words, their desire to buy from you must outweigh their hesitation.

You could say there are many variables involved in persuasion such as personality, product knowledge, and hard work, all of which are important. But when you fully examine the collective viewpoints of both buyers and sellers, all transactions ultimately boil down to four elements. These elements operate together in what I call the "persuasion equation."

THE MISSION OF THE NEXT FOUR CHAPTERS IS TO HELP YOU ESTABLISH A POSITIVE RELATIONSHIP POSITION WITH BUYERS.

*In eager pursuit of this vital business goal, the *SalesMind* answers these interlocking questions about persuasion:*

- **Connection (Chapter 5): How do you develop a *pathway* for persuasion?**

- **Value (Chapter 6): How do you fuel the *engine* of persuasion?**

- **Urgency (Chapter 7): How do you create the proper *effect* of persuasion?**

- **Leverage (Chapter 8): How do you achieve the maximum *price* from persuasion?**

The arts and skills of persuasion obviously are the heart of selling. Without a strong command of them, the other skills discussed in Parts I and III will not alone deliver maximum results. However, vital as the possession of strong persuasive ability is, it cannot reach its full potential either unless Part One's Desire and Part Three's Timing skills are fully engaged.

*Sales*Minds know that it takes all three parts functioning in smooth harmony to achieve their full potential.

5

CONNECTION

SELL YOURSELF FIRST

She was barely five feet tall. She embodied total humility. She was a poor Albanian who rejected all the wealth, recognition, and credit that poured her way. She served the needs of the poorest of the poor for generations. She was not a powerful communicator, but diplomats and heads of state came to her doorstep—if they could find her. When anyone saw her face or looked into her eyes in a magazine picture, there was an instant bond—a bond that melted arrogance and selfishness; a bond that was pure, compelling, and holy. She was a gift to humanity. She was Mother Teresa.

He also emerged from the slums to find followers in bars all over town. He studied history intently but failed to absorb its most important lessons. He was thrown in jail for inciting rebellion. In his intense and fiery speeches, he played upon the economic hardships and nationalism of his people. He commanded and received absolute loyalty, or slaughtered those who refused to give it. When you saw his eyes in a magazine picture, he was always totally engaged. He sold millions on an illusion and caused the death of thirty million people. He was the face of evil. He was Adolph Hitler.

Despite their opposite legacies, the one powerful reality these two shared was the ability to connect with millions of people.

"I never met a man I didn't like."
—— **Will Rogers**

CONNECTION IS THE PATHWAY TO PERSUASION

Connection is defined as "a union, bond, link, or relation." Connection is the relationship path that allows communication and energy to travel freely between buyer and seller. It requires a degree of bonding between people sufficient to allow for the proportional free-flow of communication and emotion. You wouldn't tell a stranger your secrets. If you connect with a buyer, you are in a position to sell. If you don't connect (or disconnect later), you don't sell. It's that simple.

A *Sales*Mind must develop these connection skills with buyers in order for this mutual rapport and trust to develop. As relationship trust is developed, the buyer is willing to spend more time to digest the value of your offer versus those of your competitors. Connection is the first of three elements that persuade buyers. The other two, Value and Urgency, are discussed in the next two chapters.

Connection is the quality and free flow of energy with minimal friction between the buyer and the seller. It's like a cord plugged into a socket allowing electricity to flow. Disconnection on the other hand, is the absence of that positive energy exchange due to friction or emotional distance.

Buyer and seller connection allows the persuasion process to move from personal indifference to trust.

ARE YOU LIKABLE?

I like you. That feeling or impression is the most powerful buying emotion that can cross a buyer's mind. Cause and effect goes on here. Buyers like you because you are *likable*. Buyers seldom verbalize how they feel about a *Sales*Mind, but the sooner they like you, the better everything goes in the sale and the relationship.

Connection is being likable for tangible reasons. Consider just the smile. Research shows that smiling at another person will light up their brain's receivers in an MRI faster than any other facial expression you can make. That's tangible. Just smile.

Are you likable? How do you know for sure? And exactly what is likable anyway? What if you *think* you're likable but really aren't to many buyers? Why would a buyer really like you and not want to do business with you? The short answers are found in these three principles:

1. ***Trust.*** A buyer must feel some level of emotional bond to establish a belief that you can be trusted.

2. ***Test.*** That trust is tested when you are compared to other sellers as the buyer seeks maximum value.

3. ***Trade.*** The buyer perceives a greater gain than the worth of the money involved by exchanging it for your value.

I met Denis Waitley in 1985 when he conducted a seminar here in Atlanta. I was fortunate to get a personally-signed copy of his classic book, *The Double Win*, in which he puts forth a key idea about the issue of connection:

"When Double Winners deal with a prospect, an adversary, or a potential friend, their attitude is service-oriented, not self-oriented. Their conversation is for the other person, not themselves. When we have other people's interests at heart, not just our own, the others can see it."
—— **Denis Waitley**

That passage clearly supports the idea that positive buyer emotions about you act as positive leverage. Remember though, it's still possible for them to like you but buy from someone else because your competitor's value is higher, or their price is cheaper.

*Buyers like a Sales**Mind.***

BEING LIKED IN SALES IS PROGRESSIVE AND REPETITIVE

Being liked is actually a process of emotion, time, and interaction. Progressive means being liked by the buyer in a way that advances and accumulates in steps over time. Repetitive means being liked by buyers through consistent interaction with them. Buyers will forget about you if you don't see them often enough. Progress in a relationship operates in three phases:

Phase One, *Immediate Connection:* The buyer likes you, doesn't like you, or never gets a full chance to like you upon first impression.

The key here is at *upon first impression.* The buyer always reacts emotionally to your first impression, whether on the phone, in a first meeting, or even in an initial email or letter. Remember that today's buyers have been hustled a lot, and they also interact with a lot of plastic people who don't have their best interests in mind.

But when connection is occurring with you, a buyer feels:

- **Non-defensive or non-threatened** because of your calming demeanor or voice.

- **Humored** because if a buyer will laugh with you, there is a special connection.

- **Impressed** because your reputation has preceded you.

- **Attentive** because of your energy and uniqueness.

- **Interested** because there are reasons for your enthusiasm, and they want to know about them.

- **Comfortable** because your presence is pleasant in their anxious day.

- **Responsive** because of your confidence, specific knowledge, and effective articulation.

- **Trusting** because of your focus on helping them instead of yourself.

- **Commonality** because you are like them or are flexible enough to find common ground and present yourself as being somewhat like them.

It is invaluable for buyers to connect with you at first impression to start the sales momentum moving toward:

Phase Two, *First-Sale Connection*: Your likability contin-ues to go up, leading to the very first sale.

This next phase validates the initial feelings the buyer had about you. They *were* right the first time. They do like you and feel they can trust you. And they trust you for what may be many reasons. The more dimensions the buyer likes about you, the more positive leverage you have in this connection process.

In this second phase, buyers move past immediate feelings about you to a more thorough assessment of who you are. They may also get feedback from their associates about you. Your connection and trust with them moves past a first impression phase to one of professional connection, that is, to connection where money, risk, and their own welfare are involved.

We can classify this second connection phase as the quality of connection up until the completion of a first or only transaction. It is crucial to sincerely sustain likability up to the first transaction, so that you can experience:

Phase Three, *Partner Connection*: Root feelings develop over time in a sustained relationship after multiple sales.

Your goal is phase three level of connection. You were liked at first for certain reasons, and you will most likely stay liked for those same reasons. In this phase, you can add the business and personal value the buyer has obtained from you to your leverage. They, the buyer's company, have a positive transaction history with you. I emphasize business value because a buyer can like you personally but will most likely do business with the ultimate seller they perceive benefits their business life the most. This becomes even truer during times when the economy tightens.

As we discussed earlier, there is also the degree of *repetition* of your presence in the connection. Like all relationships, the number and quality of the connections are directly proportional to the depth of the relationship. In this third phase, connection takes on the nature of a permanent relationship position, and both parties desire to be permanent partners.

You have now established three layers of connection: They first liked you, they bought from you (and experienced value), and now they have gotten to know you personally. Best of all, this top layer of personal connection involves the exchange of personal experiences and information. This relationship level links the personal backgrounds, families, and lives of a buyer and seller. You become true business friends. You might also become personal friends. I have a lot of personal friends that started with a business relationship.

Connection with a buyer progresses in phases over time.

CONNECTION PROBLEMS

Sometimes it is not that a buyer doesn't want to connect with you, it is just they have a combination of various daily realities blocking connection. Here, I focus attention on *you*, not on the buyer:

- **You combat numbers, chances, and timing.**

There can be difficulty in bonding with a buyer because of the reality of achieving actual contact in the first place. Buyers are out, in meetings, or otherwise unavailable.

As an average, you might get through to a desired contact between ten and forty percent of the time, depending on the relationship, circumstance, and timing. (If you have private cell phone numbers, obviously that number could be much higher, so get them whenever possible.) The low rate of successful contacts means that if you aren't making lots of appointment-setting calls, you can't generate enough potential contacts to be effective.

It's like a baseball player's batting average. To get the hits and RBI's, he has to have the at-bats. It's easy to find sales failures who didn't make it because they didn't penetrate the maze of stalls, secretaries, and voicemail screens consistently. Being successful demands that you generate the coverage (Chapter 11) required to put yourself in front of enough potential decision-makers.

- **You encounter buyer defensiveness, anxiety, or distraction.**

The unfortunate reality is that some buyers are so absorbed with their own emotions and distractions that you will never connect. Also, at times you cannot connect fast enough, or your competitor has already connected.

- **You blew your first impression.**

There is an absence of positive buyer impact by you at first contact. Your first impression conveyed in the mail, on the phone, or certainly in person, must represent the best possible you and the most sincere you. This means the best extension of your unique, individual personality and character.

You then combine that energy with a trained initial approach. You are prepared to listen and ask questions. As a matter of fact, even if you are struggling, portray yourself as a confident winner.

No one wants to do business with someone they perceive to be a loser. In this society winners are sought and valued. But regardless of success or failure, you should always have a sincere concern for the buyer. A powerful initial impression substantially increases the leverage you bring to the beginning of the sale, where momentum is critical. You never have a second chance to make a first impression.

- **You failed to determine which role to play.**

What sales role do I need to fill today in relation to this buyer and this situation? Each time you have a buyer contact, you will play a role based on the development and condition of the sale at that time. These six roles are:

1. **Interviewer.** Your role is to ask, listen, and absorb the buyers' world—their current situations, needs, and desires.

2. **Counselor.** Your role is to offer advice that relates the value of your program to a specific situation, and preferably solves one of the buyer's problems.

3. **Separator.** Your role is to differentiate yourself from the competition or from the buyer's desire to solve the problem in question internally.

4. **Presenter.** Your role is to explain the complete impact of your program in a deliberate and outlined fashion.

5. **Coach.** Your role is to help the buyer make adjustments and respond to change.

6. **Expander.** Your role is to take one of your sales concepts and elaborate on its implications and value to meet the buyer's specific need.

Become an expert on all six roles, and then carefully try to help each buyer. Don't worry, the proper role will emerge as you begin to interact with the buyer.

*A Sales**Mind** overcomes connection obstacles and plays various roles with buyers to enable effective persuasion to occur.*

CONNECT WITH A BETTER CHARACTER

Notice that the heading above is not "Connect with a Better Personality." It is possible—and fairly common—to have a wonderful personality combined with a poor character. Character is the foundation of the principles, judgment, and values upon which you operate. You can be one of many types of personalities, but those personalities should share fundamental character elements that are universally respected and responded to by others, obviously including buyers.

Do These Words Reflect Your Character?

Care
Honesty
Loyalty
Fairness
Discipline
Consistency
Truthfulness
Transparency
Responsibility
Trustworthiness

If they do, your connection with *all* people will reflect them. Your beliefs, conversation, actions, and service will be consistent with them. As a *Sales*Mind, your effectiveness in bonding with buyers is directly related to your character connection.

Character Is Easier Kept Than Restored

Do you have credible judgment?

One of the most valuable positions you can be in with a buyer at any relationship stage is for that buyer to need your experienced opinion on how to deal with a problem, situation, or gray area in their business. They are asking for your judgment call. I call it "credible judgment."

When they ask, if you are able to offer a successful solution that occurred in a related buyer experience, you establish credibility in a powerful way. Your next step is to articulate why and exactly how your solution will be successful for them, thus adding the enormous worth of judgment. This is the pinnacle of business value to the buyer, and they will pay for that value. Why? Because you bring experience, knowledge, and insights to the table that they could not assemble themselves. You must also be able to accomplish this process better than your competition if your solution judgment is compared to theirs.

A *Sales*Mind also makes every possible attempt to communicate with humble credible judgment at all times. I emphasize *humble* because some salespeople have to constantly guard against coming across as being haughty about their specialized know-how.

And be lighthearted. Even when offering a valuable judgment, a *Sales*Mind strikes a careful balance between the grim recitation of facts and examples on the one hand, and seeming to treat the buyer's problem as a joke on the other.

During a football telecast Pat Summerall and his partner, John Madden, the Hall of Fame football coach and sportscaster, were watching a running back get off to a slow first half.

"John, do you ever have slow starts?" Summerall asked Madden.

"Oh, of course I have slow starts . . . and parts, days . . . slow everything," was Madden's reply. It was spontaneous, funny, and humble. John Madden is one of the most credible and brilliant football analysts of all time. He also knows when to lighten up and laugh to connect. Laughter is the music of the soul.

*A **Sales**Mind connects with character and credible judgment to enhance buyer persuasion.*

CONNECT WITH BETTER COMMUNICATION

*Sales*Minds are not just high-character people who are likable and credible. They also generate deeper and more powerful connections within some fundamental communication rules. To connect with buyers, a *Sales*Mind must:

- Be able to communicate with energy and intensity.

- Be able to deliver information quickly for written or electronic communication. It does little to have a great story and not be able to distill and deliver it quickly. To boost your communication power—and therefore your earning power—work on brevity, pace, and tempo when presenting. A long story dies quickly these days when attention spans are short.

- Be able to blend the discussion of features with, "The value to you of . . . ."

- Be able to work on expanding vocabulary. Keep handy and use a dictionary and a thesaurus. Talk to intelligent people that have sharply defined ideas. Model them and their delivery. Watch news people and professional communicators. There are reasons why they are pros and get paid as such.

These are key communication dimensions of a *Sales*Mind who knows how to connect. This valuable skill is no accident and is substantially enhanced when it is treated as a conscious, trained communication skill.

A *Sales*Mind *communicates sharply and congruently to persuade buyers.*

CONNECT IN A SEQUENCE

All selling operates in an ongoing process or sequence of communications between buyers and sellers. Many times in the sales process, a connection sequence will repeat itself with the same buyer. This is not a sales process book, but it's key to know and apply the sequence of the following four basic elements of connection:

One: Input. This connection process skill begins in a first time meeting with a buyer. It involves questioning, and closely listening to the answers. It means focusing on, recording, writing notes, and maintaining proper body language. I call this process "input."

Look around your buyer's office—which may be a job site, their kitchen, a restaurant table—and probe lightly for a personal connection point of rapport such as family, a common associate, a current event, or a hot item in their industry. Input is your absorption of the buyer's world, and a *Sales*Mind knows that this process draws in energy and information from the buyer, the first vital component of gaining trust.

Two: Translation. The second element of connection skill involves instantaneous mental "translation" by you of buyer input. Translation is interpreting buyer expectations and objections and blending them with the value of your program instantly. You must know every aspect of your program so that you are capable of presenting under pressure or with strict time constraints.

When I first started selling copiers years ago, we would assemble in the office as a team three nights a week—after putting in a hard day's work—and practice sales interviews. During those nighttime training sessions we absorbed information that permitted us to customize demonstrations more effectively. That type of repetition and practice creates deeper program knowledge and more fluid questions for transfer into reflexive, value-based solutions. I'm thankful. There is no substitute for mental translation practice.

Three: Output. After your mental translation of buyer input, this next connection skill is your presentation of custom value, what I call "output." Can you present your program verbally, visually, and fluidly? This presentation, depending on the kind of product and the scope of sale, may have several output steps:

- Your initial presentation covering every custom point possible.

- Your digestion of the information and feedback gathered at the first meeting to present in a second presentation.

- In a large dollar or long cycle sale, this could go on for some time and involve several of these cycles: input, translate, output—input, translate, output.

Following your presentation or demonstration, of course ask for the order if the buyer is informed and the scenario is viable. You would probably also respond to an objection or two. But, barring a first-call close, you are now in a follow-up position. Are you prepared to take control of every follow-up?

Four: Reconnection. Selling involves follow-up, follow-up, and more follow-up. Switch to another career if you don't want to do it consistently, even relentlessly. Each follow-up presents an opportunity for reconnection with your buyer. It is vital to establish a specific reconnection time while with your buyer. This will set you up for the next phone call or live meeting. Before leaving your buyer:

- Direct and agree with them on the next dated action step, and make it soon. (See Action, Chapter 3) I mean "soon" as in a few days if possible, while you and your program's value are fresh in their mind. Don't let things get cold.

- Document that step in writing in front of your buyer by whipping out your planner or PDA and zeroing in on a date. That's a *Sales*Mind doing his or her job.

- Mail a personal short thank-you note that day to your buyer and watch your reconnection success skyrocket. One principle I follow is to ask myself, "How many thank-you notes can I send out?" If I can answer "a lot of them," then I know I have plentiful reasons to be thanking people. Those reasons in my world are appointments, closed sales, referrals, and higher income. What about you?

- Finally, agree on the best connection time for the call and make the call without fail at that exact time. The bottom line: You have to control the call. It's *your job* to sell. Don't give away control of the sale to the buyer. It's too fragile.

*A Sales**Mind** prepares, questions, analyzes, translates, presents, and follows-up in a powerful sequence of persuasive connection.*

Connection is the *pathway* of persuasion. Your ability to connect with buyers opens up the opportunity of your proposition for them. But once a buyer develops rapport with you and you have gained their attention, they will want something. Which brings us to why buyers buy and part with money.

VALUE

WHY BUYERS REALLY PAY MORE

Picture this: Years ago—before cell phones—you take a cross-country trip alone across the desert. At the most desolate stretch, you run out of gas and clunk off to the side of the road.

You can't believe it, but this is certainly a time to face reality. All you can see is sand and cactus all the way to the horizon in every direction.

You were in a rush when you left, so you went light on supplies. You have but a minimum amount of water, and no extra gas. But you're not worried. Surely there will be passers-by who will help.

The only person who passes by during the entire first day is a guy selling a 10-gallon tank of gas—for $2000.00. He looks like a pirate and will not rescue you or sell you anything else.

You need that gas desperately, but his predatory gouging makes you so angry that you tell him to go to the nether regions. You assume the next person who drives by will surely help; you'll get gas, you'll be given water, and you'll be able to move on. Everything will be fine.

Nobody comes for most of the second day. You are out of water and now desperate. You could die out there. As last someone appears—the gas peddler. And now his price is $5000.00. Would you pay it?

VALUE IS THE ENGINE OF PERSUASION

Value is defined as "monetary or material worth, or worth as measured in usefulness or importance, or a fair return for something." Value is the buyer's comparison of personal benefit received to the price paid. Value *powers* persuasion. So what is your product or program worth to a buyer? To answer that question, you must first consider some of these tough realities:

- **Buyers are very well trained.**

The Wal-Mart concept that they can beat your price somewhere else permeates the thinking of today's buyers.

Some buyers automatically tell all sellers they can buy whatever is being offered for less because many sellers immediately lower their price without further pressure.

Can your buyer really get your total program cheaper? And better? Is the lower price they would pay your competitor their only cost? Do you have to give away the profit in the sale to close it?

I ask every attendee in my sales seminars, "Is the buyer better trained in resistance than you are in persuasion?" Think about that.

- **The cost to everyone of giving away money.**

Sellers don't want to give away their profits, but it's done every day. Unfortunately, many salespeople offer to sell for less at the first sign of price resistance. Fear of losing the sale makes them think, "Why not give away some profit and just bring this business in?" This attitude puts heavy downside pressure on prices for all competitors; everybody in that particular field then faces a tougher task in maintaining profitability.

- **Value is belief on the part of the seller and perception on the part of the buyer.**

First, a buyer must believe in, and be able to validate, that what they're being offered is worth the extra money. Sellers seeking profitable sales must have better trained people, a better service program, and testimonials from happy buyers to support their position.

Second, A *Sales*Mind must be able to generate in the buyer's mind a clear, advantageous perception of comparative value (versus the competition) to accomplish persuasion.

- **Worth over sacrifice.**

If a *Sales*Mind does not have an offering of inherent or added value greater in importance than the buyer's perceived value of their money, then the *Sales*Mind will not earn the buyer's money.

- **Value is multi-dimensional.**

Value has different dimensions, each impacting a buyer's perception in its own way. The key is for the total value perception to be strong enough to tilt (leverage) a decision to transact your way, and at the best possible margin. Those value dimensions are:

- *Universal* **Value**
- *Specific Business* **Value**
- *Personal Life* **Value**
- *Credibility* **Value**
- *Uniqueness* **Value**

You must understand and articulate all of these value dimensions with the buyer to enhance their value perception.

In persuasion, a buyer's value perception is a *Sales****Mind****'s value position.*

UNIVERSAL VALUE

"You can get anything you want in life if you will help enough other people get what they want."
—— **Zig Ziglar**

Every human being wants to *feel good* and *reduce pain*. They buy products and services that possess the ability to make those contributions. I call this "Universal Value," and this is the platform on which a *Sales*Mind operates in their dealings with buyers. Buyers spend money (which incurs risk) and implicitly say to the seller, ***"I will spend money if you will help me to…***

feel safer
be more loved
reduce my costs
alleviate my pains
make more money
improve my health
gain more confidence
attract more attention
have a better family life
save and use time wisely
get more affection from others
become happier in my life and job
enhance my sense of security with God
ease my fears about today and the future
achieve greater appreciation and recognition

Cut through all the smiles, armor, and plastic with people, and you'll discover that what most people want in life can be found somewhere in the bell-shaped figure above. Not everyone feels the need for all of them all the time, and some of the desires listed are not necessarily the proper things to seek. However, buyers of all kinds are spending vast sums of money to feed those desires.

SalesMinds persuade buyers with value propositions for reducing pain and increasing gain.

SPECIFIC BUSINESS VALUE (SBV)

Specific Business Value is the exact combination of value experiences that a buyer gets from a transaction with your company involving you, the product, the program, and all service aspects. It is the anchor of the value experience.

The role of the *Sales*Mind in helping contribute SBV is based on possessing answers to the four fundamental questions regarding buyer choice, buyer spending, buyer perception, and buyer viewpoint:

One: What Choices Does a Buyer Have?

- They can buy from you (excellent).
- They can buy from your competitor (not so excellent).
- They can postpone the decision, possibly for a long time.
- They can do the job internally.
- They can cancel the job and save the money.

So, let's take a look at why buyers spend money so that you become their choice:

Two: What Are the Basic Reasons Why a Buyer Spends Money?

- To make more money than the expenditure.

- To reduce costs above the expenditure.

- To make their own (or their employees) life easier and more satisfying.

- To save or reallocate time.

A *Sales*Mind must align those reasons with buyer perception.

Three: How Does the Seller Test If the Buyer Is Perceiving Value?

A seller must be able to answer value questions from the buyer's perspective. If a customer has paid you before, that value perception is based on *reflection*. If a prospect has never bought from you, that value perception is based on *anticipation*.

Your presentation and position with the buyer should be able to pass "the value test" on the next page, which is focused on buyer perception. Remember, it's not what you say or how you say it. What matters is how your communication is perceived.

The Value Test

Are you perceived to be valuable to a buyer because you are or will become:

- A direct asset to produce revenue, profits, cash flow, and transactions for them?
- A helper with their marketability, market access, promotion, and advertising?
- An asset to help them ingest and manage change to advantage?
- A partner who is able to reduce their risks, costs, and add efficiency?
- A problem-solver, case-analyzer for them?
- An aid to their leadership, future position, and vision?
- An asset in helping their staff people to be more effective and productive?
- A connecting point of your own management and staff to them?
- A contributor to the positive emotional climate of their business?
- An influence to increase the effectiveness of their communications?
- A source to increase the effectiveness of their information management?
- A partner to help them conduct faster business?
- A source of knowledge to help in their decision-making?
- A public relations or image-enhancer for them?
- An element to add worth for their owners, investors, or shareholders?

If you can honestly say you are even asking, let alone answering these questions in an affirmative way, you understand what it will take to become a value-added *Sales*Mind.

One of my clients, a Fortune Two Hundred company, needed to stop and then reverse their eroding leverage so they could enhance their value position. Nothing less than achieving this company-wide would enable them to increase their prices and margins.

To accomplish that objective, we rolled out a customized version of my *Sales*Mind training model in two of their divisions, district by district. We did workshops with managers, salespeople, and staff people to get tough answers that could be communicated within the organization and to buyers. Some of the value questions we answered and then implemented were:

- Do you believe that you are worth the price you are asking for?
- Why exactly (every day) are you valuable to your buyers?
- Are you prepared to render the service necessary to command higher prices?
- What is your first immediate action to improve your daily performance?

Not only have these workshops produced immediate results and continue to have a tremendous financial impact for my client, but they have also enhanced the lives of many of the attendees. I get a constant stream of letters and emails from employees who want to lead and be of value, and who want to possess personal and team leverage. They wanted to reach their value objectives quickly, and they have achieved them. What about you?

Four: How Does the Customer's Viewpoint Differ from the Prospect's Viewpoint Regarding Value?

Customers. Because of their transaction history with you, they are already experiencing some sense of value, low or high. They can reflect on it. That positive value must be maintained and accelerated because the customer will continuously evaluate its worth in relation to their price position with you.

Prospects. With no history with you, prospects merely have a sense of anticipated value that is perceived to take place after the first transaction. To leverage that buyer perception and confidence, ask yourself:

- How much of my information has my buyer absorbed?
- How much of that information has value?
- How much time so far have I spent with decision-makers?
- How much competition is in this proposal equation?
- How much desire do I discern in the buyer for us to be their sole source of supply?

I understand that a buyer takes a risk in buying from me for the first time. To overcome this, I must expend extra effort to sell first-time buyers.

How much desire have I placed in the buyer's mind for us to be their unique source or solution? Since there is no established reference point of history with you, they will ask questions:

- What is your product or service?
- What will it do, and how does your program work?
- What will it do for me?
- How can you prove your claims?
- Who besides you says your program is great?

Later on in this chapter, we will examine in more detail these credibility value issues.

Prospects who ask these questions must perceive value through their connection with you, through their examination of your satisfied buyers, through the tailored benefits of your offering in a presentation, and through the persistence of your follow-up to earn their business.

Creating strong value perception in prospects to buy only from you—and to buy from you now—is one of the most powerful skills a *Sales*Mind can possess.

For persuasion to occur, a buyer must perceive that they will experience specific business value.

PERSONAL LIFE VALUE

The answer to the following question is all that ultimately matters to a buyer: *How does my relationship with you help me in my personal life?* Please, anyone, prove me wrong about making this assertion. I've issued that challenge many times—with no takers.

Most buyers work to live, not live to work. The ultimate goal of any business transaction is to enhance the customer's personal emotional quality of life, period. A buyer's life is their play (not to sound too Shakespearian), and their business with you is just one minor scene from one act of that play.

This element of knowledge put into sales action is what separates a *Sales*Mind from the rest of the herd. You are presented with two intense challenges:

1. **Gathering.**

You must research, gather, ask about, investigate, and assemble a complete personal profile in a written record on every customer and prospect. That information must involve family, travels, habits, likes, dislikes, and associations as a base of understanding what that buyer desires. You have to either acquire this data from direct conversations with your buyer or get it from asking staff people that work for them.

2. **Delivering.**

You must then articulate that their desires for personal value will be enhanced both by buying from you, and from the impact of your product or service.

Let's take a closer look. Remember our elements of universal value? Take one of your top customers and use the following grid to rate how much you think transactions involving your product or service are delivering value into their personal life.

To increase the accuracy of your evaluation, consider each element and assign a rating to it before going on to the next item.

True *Sales*Minds not only know persuasion skills and fully understand their product and services, but they also sincerely know and care about their buyers. If you have this deep knowledge of your buyers, they will share personal values with little or no resistance.

You may never know your impact unless you directly ask a buyer about it, or you may say, "My product is just an office widget." But in relative terms to the potential of your product, give the following exercise a shot. You'll be glad you did when you see your increased income and success:

My Program's Effect on Aspects of My Buyer's Personal Life:

Buyers' Personal Value Gained	Effect Rating*
Making more take-home money	_____
Reducing budget costs	_____
Reducing pains affecting how they feel away from work	_____
Reducing fears to lower anxiety	_____
Becoming more loved by those in their personal life	_____
Getting more attention	_____
Becoming more appreciated	_____
Feeling safer	_____
Being healthier	_____
Being happier daily away from work	_____
Having a better family life	_____
Acquiring future benefits for their children	_____
Having more personal confidence	_____
Feeling more secure with God	_____
Total	_____

* Effect Rating. Assign a value ranging from 0 for no effect to 12 for High Effect.

- How are you doing personally with this buyer?
- What are your total numbers in the fourteen categories?
- What is your average?

- Do you believe you are contributing value to your buyer's personal life?
- How much do you sincerely care about your buyer?
- How well do you know your buyer?

Remember this personal value experienced by the buyer is mostly a by-product of specific business value generated for the buyer through a business relationship. And again, you have to solicit and fashion a customer profile to tailor value in business to their life circumstances.

The deepest buyer persuasion is accomplished when specific business value migrates into the effect of personal life value.

CREDIBILITY VALUE

The *Sales*Mind is obsessed with the *credibility* dimension of value. Credibility means objective, outside corroboration of the value of your program as observed or experienced by satisfied buyers. It may also mean an outside neutral party, such as a research company, or a professional business association validating that you are the best.

Remember the *Good House Keeping Seal of Approval?* Do you read *Consumer Reports?* I'm sure you've seen companies brag on TV about winning the *Malcolm Baldridge Quality Award.* You get the idea. It's powerful persuasion.

This presentation of credibility closes the perception gap the buyer faces between claim and truth. Credibility removes *doubt*, the biggest stumbling block to a sale. Remember your credible judgment? This integrity supports that judgment as an extremely valuable asset.

Your credibility also reduces the buyers' fears, perceived risks, and unknown outcomes. You are offering independently known information on your company, which is very powerful. This information and communication ratchets the mind of the prospect to the next step of interest in you. They are curious to see how your credibility value creates a solution for their next business problem or situation. You are a counselor-seller, which is just like being a sales doctor.

Increase Your Credibility with the Buyer

Buyers today crave to do business with credible sellers because they have been let down, hustled, and burnt so many times. You can change that skepticism by providing these two valuable elements:

- **Expert status.**

A *Sales*Mind gains credibility by constantly expanding their expertise of product, industry, competition, and market to validate the buyer's need for them and their product only. There is only one way to gain this level of confidence: You have to self-train in a fast-paced learning program by reading, updating, interviewing, experimenting, outlining, and organizing the mass of your product's meaning.

Convert that data into a crystal-clear message of how its value exceeds a buyer's expectations. This is vital to sales success. The buyer moves toward trust when the

*Sales*Mind can clearly offer solution-centered judgment for a need, problem, or situation in their business.

- **Proof.**
Your credibility is most powerfully impacted by testimonials, customer surveys, statistics, referrals, quotations, case studies, and examples of those business successes that happened to one of your buyers because of your program. Nothing is as powerful as proof to support your sales claims of helping buyers make money, reduce costs, solve problems, feel better, and make their lives easier.

Credibility value is the objectivity factor in buyer persuasion.

UNIQUENESS VALUE

Consider and put in perspective the unique type of value associated with some of these examples in their time:

- Elvis in the music world.
- Microsoft in the computer world.
- The Seven Wonders of the Ancient World.
- The individuality of each of your kids.
- The Bible in the literature or religious world.

The impact of all these examples is unified by one variable: They all have a high *uniqueness* factor of value. They all are or were perceived as different in people's minds.

What about you? Are you really any different in your buyer's mind than any of your competitors? Are your company's services or products really better? Are you individually as a *Sales*Mind really any better and contribute any more value than another vendor? If your claims of uniqueness and differentiation are really true, you have to communicate and substantiate them.

The most potent degree of value with the most leverage is uniqueness. Uniqueness value is positioning yourself, your company, and your program as special, better, and different. Can you generate the persuasion power to be a unique consideration?

Our lives today in America have become so full of the common and the mass-produced. It's what I call the "Wal-Mart mentality." We are often so group-oriented, so identified with the herd. As a contrast, whether or not you are a Rush Limbaugh fan, I respect the fact that he talks consistently about being a unique thinking individual, not a hostage to yours or a group's feelings.

Where is your uniqueness? Where is your differentiation? How do you know? You can possess uniqueness value to a buyer by:

- Doing your work in a different and special way to gain their attention.
- Extending yourself with out-of-the-box thinking, and by avoiding mundane and boringly ordinary sales terms. That is where your maximum potential lies.
- Utilizing the power of the right first impression.
- Being a personal marketer beyond the simple value of the product.

- Making your sales business and approach fun and compelling for the buyer.
- Documenting those unique things you did with your best sale ever.

Your product may be exactly like another seller's. So any uniqueness value perception by the buyer of you adds to exclusivity. Unique buyer perception is enhanced by the total impact of your talent, plus your personality, and plus the mix of services offered by you and your company. Make sure you tailor and implement these unique aspects within your selling approach:

Communicate Your Uniqueness Through:

First impression

Imagination

Creativity

Differentiation

Customized testimonials

Personality into the sale

Custom service components

Special intellectual capital

Consultation

Separation

Finding and exploiting a niche

Combining several angles into a compelling blend

Using and being aware of humor at all times

Applying credible judgment in a better way

So resolve to be unique. Then engrave these two *Sales*Mind concepts on your own mind and become skilled at driving uniqueness value into the buyer's mind:

1. Either your product, program or service level is truly different, exclusive, or has limited access, which is enormous leverage, OR—

2. You have strong personal connection skills that help to create a better perception of common variables in the buyer's mind about your product or program's uniqueness.

*A **Sales**Mind establishes uniqueness value to gain a position of difference in the buyer's thinking.*

Value is the *engine* of persuasion. Yet there is one more bridge to cross to attain the kind of position with the buyer that will yield a transaction at a fair price. Listen up, because you can't miss this next element of persuasion that accelerates buyers toward you.

7

URGENCY

I WANT TO BUY IT NOW

Every parent of one of this generation's kids knows about this: At first you hear about it on the parent grapevine. Then you see the story on TV. Johnny comes home and says everyone at school is talking about it and getting one for Christmas. You think, "Oh no, not me. I can't believe anybody is dumb enough to wait in line for one of those." Then Erma next door calls and says, "Did you get one yet? I did. I got one."

Erma is about to get a leg up on you? No way. You call your local Toys R Us and they have been out for over a week. You start to panic. You call around to every toy store and everybody is out. Everybody. How are you going to let Johnny down? Christmas is only a week away. You go on eBay and price a few. At $89.00. That's highway robbery. You start to sink into depression that you are a negligent parent. You can't sleep the next two nights.

You get a call from a friend at church on your cell phone the next day and it's marked "urgent." She just found a Target store where a small shipment just came in, and the line is building. You drop your work, fly out of the office, meet your friend, and proceed to wait two hours to finally secure the Holy Grail.

No, it's not the Holy Grail, it's a Tickle Me Elmo. But you got one. Johnny will think you are a miracle worker. The day is saved. American marketing has created a sense of urgency: you have to have a toy that you never conceived you would fall for. Johnny plays with Elmo for six days. Oh well.

What's this got to do with being a *Sales*Mind? Everything. The goal is for a perception to occur of immediate desire for the buyer to have your product or program. Sometimes it is just the buyers' desire for your product that creates urgency, but most often you have to persuade. Your goal is to affect a sense of urgency in the buyer to transact with you now.

URGENCY IS THE EFFECT OF PERSUASION

Urgency is defined as "requiring immediate action." The following subject of buyer urgency is very touchy. It deals with the fine line of helping versus pushing buyers. Many of my peers will not even deal with it, let alone train or write about it. But I will, and have for years. The reason is because of our focus on the fragility of the buyer's welfare (and rightly so). We believe that trying to affect their motivation to buy now might collide with this reverent view of them. So as a result, we don't persist as we should. A *Sales*Mind must internalize these two rules about urgency:

The buyer needs a disturbing problem. If a legitimate buyer will not buy, they are either unaware of their problem, or just not sufficiently disturbed by it yet. It is the job of the *Sales*Mind to sufficiently disturb the buyer with their (own) real problem, and then help them act on solving that problem now.

The seller (you) provides a better choice. In business, there is a fundamental friction (sometimes very small) between the buyer and seller. The seller always wants to make a sale now when the buyer is informed, but often times the buyer wants to shop around, wait, or just go away and not be bothered by the *Sales*Mind. The buyer somehow believes that by waiting and buying time, they will make a better decision, find a better product, and maybe spend less. That rationale is understandable, but it has (potentially) some false assumptions. Either way, the *Sales*Mind needs to keep that reality in perspective.

A *Sales*Mind needs to assess and then attempt to stimulate urgency because buyers also say, "I'll get back to you" and don't. Every buyer says it. It's easy and reflexive. They can part company with you at will. A buyer simply loses emotional urgency (and then they can vanish into the arms of the competition).

Do all of your buyers respond to your propositions with immediate action? I didn't think so. Don't you wish they would? Of course. You can influence their response now by impacting the urgency variable in their mind. You may also determine it can't be impacted right now, call back on them later, and move on.

Are You Afraid of the Buyer?

You shouldn't be. As a *Sales*Mind, the fundamental questions to think through and ask yourself for each buyer situation are:

- Am I pushing the buyer to buy now because of my own agenda? Am I truly helping the buyer to act more urgently to buy because I believe the purchase will help them now?

- Do I realize that buyers primarily care about their own urgency drivers, not mine?

- Am I afraid the buyer will feel I'm pushy even when they don't feel I am?

- If I operate with this fear of being pushy, am I missing many current transaction opportunities? Should I perhaps consider another career that is more comfortable?

- Am I connected to the buyer and prepared with skill to accelerate the buyer's urgency without them getting defensive?

- Am I afraid to be rejected or to lose this deal because I need the income (commission) from it?

- Do I respect my own ability to help the buyer make a better, more well-informed decision now? While things are fresh in their mind, am I capable of eliminating the attrition of information they will experience while things cool off?

- Do I understand that an urgent attitude is a huge contribution in amassing achievements of any kind?

- What do I do when a buyer looks me right in the eye and says, "We're going to think on this while we shop around, and we'll get back to you." Have I ever responded with a soft reflexive question such as, "Have you considered the reasons why it may be a good idea for you to think about going ahead now?"

> *"I believe that sales time invested is deserving of a present consideration of value received."*
> —— **Doug Trenary**
> "The Golden Rules of Buyer Urgency"

Before we go any further, our continued discussion of urgency must be based on the following rules of buyer welfare and consideration. I call them "The Golden Rules of Buyer Urgency." As a *Sales*Mind, I must assess as early as possible that I have:

- A fully informed buyer, or one whom I will fully inform, on the features and related value contributions of my program.

- A buyer with a need that would be fitting for a present transaction.

- A buyer who has money and is qualified and capable of authorizing a transaction.

- A buyer who just needs to tell me the truth about their situation so as to save everyone's time.

If those four criteria are met, I have an obligation to develop the urgency in my buyer to act now. If not, I will determine when the criteria are met and proceed from there. Communicate these ideas in a sincere way, and you will find less stress within the buying atmosphere.

In persuasion, a SalesMind is concerned about buyers and sincerely helps them eliminate problems and realize their desires now.

DOES THE BUYER NEED YOUR PERSUASION?

Every ultimate transaction has a combination of two buyer urgencies: Urgency in the buyer *before* your influence and urgency *after* your influence. This is a critical set of concepts to understand and react to as a seller.

Before Your Persuasion

A buyer has a need, sees an ad, and they are moved to transact solely on their own motivation. In effect, *they* supply 100% of the urgency to pay their money. The ad was the cost of generating that urgency to buy now, and your *Sales*Mind persuasion is not needed.

After Your Persuasion

Reality, most of the time, is that a buyer is self-motivated to shop your product and price it with your competition. Their existing urgency to buy now must be supplemented with *your* persuasion to inform, compare, and compel. In effect, the combined urgencies in the buyer's mind are represented by the variables below added together to equal 100%:

The beginning percentage of emotional urgency generated to buy a product is initiated by the buyer of their own free will and absent from you. Let's say that's 40% of the total urgency needed.

The remaining percentage, 60%, required for them to buy your product now must be generated as a result of the interaction and persuasion of the seller, you.

This is an arbitrary mathematical view of urgency, but it defines the atmosphere of urgency. The two urgency types must equal 100% in order to compel the buyer to buy from you now at your price.

Urgency Perspective

A *Sales*Mind with buyer connection and an offering of value must be able to recognize and intensify the state of urgency. You want them to transact in the certainty of the present, not the uncertainty of the future.

A *Sales*Mind knows the highest signal of perceived value in the buyer is the desire to transact now.

A *Sales*Mind always operates with an intelligent but not reckless or desperate sense of urgency. This means simply that the urgency approach is well thought out and prepared.

A *Sales*Mind presents thoroughly in order to paint a sufficiently disturbing problem so that the buyer's perspective says: "I must fix this problem NOW."

*A Sales**Mind** determines how much urgency exists in the buyer to buy now and then supplies the rest of the persuasion needed to transact.*

CREATING BUYER URGENCY CAN BE TOUGH

It is not easy to generate urgency in a buyer that did not originally have it before they met you. Why is that? Let's create some answers by recognizing and examining the tough challenges in generating buyer urgency.

"Degree of Difficulty" in a Transaction

In Olympic diving, and many other sports, the final score of each competitor is based on the degree of difficulty of their performance. Only those divers who choose to perform dives with a high degree of difficulty—and do them successfully—have a realistic prospect of accumulating enough points to win a Gold Medal.

It's the same in assessing potential transactions. You want to go for the highest scores—in terms of sales revenue potential and margin—right? Here's a guide— arranged from easy to hard, that is from lowest to highest score—to help you assess the difficulty of establishing urgency in the following scenarios:

Easy (No Medal). A close emotional relationship exists between you and the buyer. These are your business friends. Other transactions in the easy group are those where the buyer needs your unique product or service now, with or without you. Such buyers are under their own urgency to make a transaction, and are willing to pay the maximum price.

Somewhat Easy (Bronze Medal). Closing under the circumstance of a sales promotion, planned discount by management, or from customers pre-sold by advertising. All these scenarios merely call for taking orders versus employing persuasion.

Hard (Silver Medal). Closing under the circumstance of a small concession of price, service, or material in return for a decision now. The trade is the buyer's decision now for some form of commensurate money or service (buy now or miss the deal). The seller has to carefully evaluate which urgency concessions are win/win and meet profit expectations of management.

Hardest (Gold Medal—You get the gold and pocket the maximum income). Closing under the circumstance of pure perceived value in the buyer. This urgency is big league. There are no price or program concessions because the seller helps generate a strong sense of urgency in the buyer. They persuade their buyers to ask themselves questions like this: "Why would I wait to defer these benefits?" In reverse, there may also be an emotional climate (assisted by you) in the buyer that they have perceived loss or pain by not having the product now. They lose by waiting one moment. This is a 9.9 judges score that puts you on the center platform!

Four Reasons Why Buyers Don't Want to Buy Now

1. The Overuse Challenge. Urgency is overused in marketing: "Today only. Limited time offer. You must act now. Closeout sale while supplies last. Buy now. Sale ends at midnight tonight."

Often, this is done ineptly, as when a sign proclaims, "Special discount today only" and the sign has been hanging in the window so long that it's faded and warped. As a buyer in this society, you have been exposed to all the tricks, and you say, "I'm not falling for that one." However, the truth is, this system works much of the time.

This marketing system of generating sales now is the most powerful there has ever been on earth. However, the pervasive overuse of urgency in promotion is a variable that certainly can make a buyer defensive or suspicious. Because buyers are so used to being jammed to buy today, a *Sales*Mind has to balance that condition with the reality that urgency is a critical element in sales transactions.

2. The Attention Challenge. It's hard to gain buyers' attention and keep them attentive in the urgent state of mind necessary to get the purchase completed. Urgency toward acting in your favor in the mind of the buyer normally is fleeting, sporadic, and inconsistent. Why? Because of the volume of stimuli, considerations, and decisions they experience in their business and personal lives.

You're not being snubbed personally when they insist on deferring a decision on your proposal until later. Often they'll say, "Because some other things have come up," or give some other vague excuse.

It can be frustrating. You presented well, they're hot to buy, supposedly ready to decide—and then their urgency suddenly fades (as does their perceived value). When this happens—and it will many times in your sales career— never take the naïve and counterproductive attitude that you have been treated badly. Simply switch on persistence and begin working the follow-up. Based on how successful you are at talking to or getting back in front of the decision-maker, the urgency may reappear.

Be Aware of These Keys in Keeping a Buyer Urgent:

- The buyers' intensity of urgency is a function of how high the value of your offering ranks on a potential customer's priority list at the time you cross his or her path. This is the "front or back burner" factor.

- The degree of competition to your proposal is crucial. Attention paid to your offering is in direct proportion to any appealing competitive relationships or activities that exist.

- Early in the connection, find out by asking where your offering is at this time on the buyer's decision-making totem pole.

- Also ask about any timing issues that might affect urgency. Could any variable or influence contribute to accelerating the urgency to decide from later to now?

3. The Distance Challenge. As we discussed in Chapter 5, Connection, the percentage of times you can get through to someone who can decide today is already low even when they are local.

That's why every element of potential impact, such as phone calls, voice mails, letters, emails, and advertising must be loaded with some reason to act now. Thus all these messages must carry your "urgency commercial" in addition to whatever else they tell the customer.

The urgency commercial must be both consistent in thrust and varied in tactic. Your challenge is proportionately increased when you are dealing with out-of-town decision-makers where you can't (with ease or at low cost) get in front of them, or with a decision-maker who always screens you with one or more secretaries, thus inserting physical and emotional distance into the scenario.

4. The Influence Challenge. You must attempt to deal with a decision-maker to compel the urgency to transact. The quality and speed of urgency to transact a decision descends from a top decision-maker a lot faster than it ascends from those below.

Every level of authority or obstruction between you and the top dog dilutes transaction urgency with their urgency agenda. Basically, they will try to control the speed of the transaction for their own reasons. That's why the cardinal rule of influence is to *start at the top*, whenever possible. This takes a little toughness and some tact, but it's worth it.

*A SalesMind **understands the difficulty factors and reasonable challenges of why buyers may have low urgency.***

THE BUYER'S B.O.I.T.

The buyer has a simple focus: What is the **Benefit of Immediate Transaction** to me? What benefit do I get from buying now as opposed to waiting? I know the emotional realm of waiting to decide. But do I know the emotions I am going to feel if I move ahead and buy now from you?

This is how a buyer thinks and feels about a transaction, particularly the first one with you. A buyer can measure the value of their cash, but can they justify and measure the impact and risk of parting with that cash to buy something from you? Why buy now?

To respond to these issues, it is vital for you to identify and intensify the two types of B.O.I.T., which are urgencies that will move a buyer in your direction:

"Natural" Urgencies are already in the buyer's mind before meeting you. These urgencies are built-in, conscious, and pre-existing. These natural urgencies to buy may be one-time or repetitive. The buyer's own position advances by buying a program in your category. They believe time is *not* on their side to defer a buying decision. They are compelled to buy now because of any of the following:

- Desire to eliminate immediate pain or solve a current problem.
- Need to have your service because of its value in satisfying their desires.
- Competitive pressure or disadvantage they are experiencing.
- Deadline for a decision they have to make.
- Seasonal variable that would motivate a purchase.
- Planning need for their organization.
- Sales needed immediately (that your program would help create).
- Installation issues for their own customers.
- Raw material of yours needed in a time-sensitive production process.
- Event-oriented consideration.
- Budget or fiscal deadline they are facing.
- Effect caused by a personal transfer, family-move, or vacation.
- Marketing campaign or product launch that is pending.

- Committee recommendation or board meeting that is coming up soon.
- Tax/fiscal year deadline requirement.
- Satisfaction issues of their own customers' needs.
- Hiring or firing moves that affect the company.

You should have a questioning track that inquires about and discovers any of these natural urgencies so you can factor them into your sales dialogue and responses. Every one you learn about is leverage on your side to stimulate urgency for an immediate transaction.

"Enhanced" Urgencies are those that have to be stimulated, enhanced, or created with your help. In other words, the buyer does not have a high degree of conscious, built-in urgency prior to your influence. They do not perceive yet that they would benefit by making a transaction now. They simply do not feel the desire to buy now. They believe time *is* on their side to stall, look around, and negotiate. To overcome these negative (to your sale) pressures, you have to add to natural urgency the remaining percent of persuasion in the buyer by:

- Emotionally intensifying any variable in the Natural Urgency list.
- Discovering and stimulating an urgency variable also not on the list.
- Firmly generating a limited financial offer or availability unknown to them at contact.
- Heightening extra pain awareness of their current condition without your product.
- Highlighting benefits unperceived initially about your product.

- Creating awareness that time to decide is really not on their side.
- Performing a presentation with perceived value that is head and shoulders above the competition.
- Enlightening an unknown market or economic variable that compels a decision.
- Articulating the purchase value of how their friend or another buyer benefited now.
- Heightening awareness of a statistical analysis of performance in your favor.

The successful application of any enhanced urgency approach requires diligent thought, planning, and effective presentation with careful dialogue. Remember, the basis of these approaches is to raise the level of urgency above that which existed before your persuasion.

*A **Sales**Mind focuses on the most important aspect of urgency: the perceived value in the buyer's mind of transacting now.*

DO YOU HAVE A SENSE OF URGENCY?

Let's shift from buyer urgency to *your* urgency. I call it "self-urgency." If you don't have urgency, how do you expect the buyer to? Self-urgency is your level of personal desire to be successful, help buyers, and see transactions get finalized. It is the mindset of realizing that time is limited to achieve results.

I recently received a letter from a commercial construction salesperson who attended one of my *Sales*Mind seminars. Instead of just going back after the program to business as usual and forgetting what he had learned, he decided to take some immediate action and apply some urgency with his other seminar-acquired skills. As he wrote here, it paid off:

"Approximately one week after attending your *Sales*Mind seminar, I again targeted a large competitive community project in the Valleydale area for our company's products. But this time I intensified my value-added sales approach. These actions netted me first a sale involving one of their houses, and then I went on to increase this entire project to a revenue level of about $100,000 per year for the next several years."

Not bad. You can also get this level of results if you are urgent. A fascinating side effect of this attitude is that your urgency will often rub off onto a buyer to also be urgent. Their attention to the transaction heightens. If you have self-urgency, you will execute business without hesitation. Your urgency will be both *intense* and *effective*.

The Intensity of Your Actions

Urgency is first generated in a sales career or specific transaction by the intensity of the desire of the *seller* to succeed. This is personal desire in motion and is a clear by-product of your defined values, goals, and desires. The level of your personal desire to fulfill a deal or make a call always has some proportional corresponding effect on the customer or prospect's urgency. It's not always noticeable, but the effect is there in some way. This self-urgency speaks to the *Sales*Mind in the silent voice: "I must, I will, I have to."

One of the most powerful mottos ever that clearly describes the intensity of one's own action is, "Lead, follow, or get out of the way." This is the kind of drive a *Sales*Mind possesses to achieve *now*. They have a profile that is easy to spot.

What about your intensity? Would you say these words and phrases describe you?

> *Desire*
> *Want to, have to, must, can't be stopped*
> *Enthusiastic persistence*
> *Diligence*
> *High energy (but always under control)*
> *Drive*
> *Passion*
> *Problem-Solver*

The Effectiveness of Your Work (with SPEED)

If you are *just* intense, your urgency can have sloppy, hurried results; the proverbial bull in the china shop effect. Your self-urgency must also generate quality, accurate, and effective work. True effectiveness is the accomplishment of priorities with SPEED (and without mistakes).

Effectiveness with speed is critical to high performance. Look at any success model today and you will see speed as a primary skill or advantage. Behind the speed, you will also see the desire by managers, coaches, and leaders to hire players and employees—at almost any cost—who can produce great results fast. This scenario also describes a *Sales*Mind. Due to their intensity, they work quickly and accurately. Speed is simply a huge advantage in any function if accuracy is maintained.

However, speed at the cost of accuracy creates some degree of net loss, which if great enough, overcomes the advantage of the speed. Bill Parcells, famous NFL coach, has said many times, "In a big game, the team with the least mistakes and turnovers will win." He's highly respected, and he's usually right. So develop your own version of intense and effective "speed selling."

*A Sales**Mind** operates with an intense sense of urgency that influences buyer persuasion in effective ways.*

Urgency is the *effect* of persuasion. But is an urgent perception of value in the buyer the end goal? Venture on and discover the answer by examining the one common condition of top performers in any vocation.

LEVERAGE

WHAT TIGER WOODS HAS

T he USA Today sports headline read, "Golf Date With Tiger Woods Goes for $425,000.00." That was the eBay auction price a round of golf fetched within minutes from a buyer with two buddies after Tiger Woods won his third Masters in 2002. It was his second back-to-back. Why the huge amount? It's financial leverage for the sellers of Tiger, or the price generated by the level of demand for him.

CBS had a rating share of 12.9, its third-best Masters ratings ever—behind only Tiger's two other

Masters victories. In his first Masters victory in 1997, the tournament also got an all-time high rating of 15.8. Consider that in 2000 a similar auction to play with Woods brought in $204,000. So two more Masters victories more than doubled that amount. (At this writing, he also just won the 2002 U.S. Open so that number is going up again.)

Tiger Woods has the position of creating proven TV viewers and ratings when he plays golf. The money is *relative* to that position. His dominance simply generates the complete attention of the entire golfing world. That makes the four hundred twenty five grand a drop in the financial golfing/TV ocean. Tiger's price in his competitive market is relative to his value.

- Why do you go to the convenience store even though you pay more?
- Why can Paul McCartney sell out any arena anywhere?
- Why does your electricity get cut off if you don't pay your bill?

These are all questions that demonstrate how leverage operates. Leverage is *position*. It is the power struggle of supply and demand. We see this power struggle in all arenas of life—in war, politics, sports, entertainment, and in day-to-day living. When you are the desired supply as a seller, buyers will pay up quickly. Most importantly, they desire to transact with you, and will pay a premium price because they benefit from doing so. Let's answer the previous questions:

- The convenience store has the position of being in a location that is close to you. You can just zip in and grab what you want, usually with no lines. But you pay more.
- Paul McCartney has the position of being a living Beatle with so many hits that promoters will pay him just about anything to tour. At this writing, his band just had the highest grossing concert tour of the year at 54.5 million dollars.
- You do not have the position to buy electricity anywhere you want or to operate without it. So pay up or get cut off.

"Do you see a man skilled in his work? He will not serve before obscure men."

"From the strength of an ox comes an abundant harvest."

—— **Proverbs**

LEVERAGE IS THE PRICE OF PERSUASION

Leverage is defined as "the action or mechanical advantage of a lever or positional advantage." Acquiring and then exerting leverage is a timeless element of business success. Leverage in sales means selling from a position of strength that is a *by-product* of being valuable.

Since age twenty-five, I have been professionally speaking and training and have developed a business that takes me all over North America serving customers. My primary business goal is to help companies and individuals sell, serve, and manage more effectively. One of my passions has always been to identify and articulate what the great companies and individual performers of our time and past times have in common.

This book is devoted to the many things those select groups do, but the one thing that is common to them all is what they possess. They possess *leverage*, a position of strength. Buyers respect that type of strength in a seller, and they will pay a fair price for it. When a buyer really wants you, they will pay more because they gain more.

In my consultations and seminars, I focus on persuading my clients (listeners) to think about every possible thing they need do to have positive leverage with their buyers. I have them define the specific components of value that make them the supply for their client's demand.

It is critical to realize that it is the seller's passion for excellence, contribution of value, and delivery of service that compel the buyer to exclusively want them. Just them. That position of strength must be earned.

In sales, you want a leveraged position when it comes to a purchase decision. That means you have done your work to position the value of your program.

The fulcrum is the transaction. Your weight (supply) is on one end of the lever with a value proposition, and the buyer's weight (demand) is on the other end with money and needs.

Make sure your price is worth your weight. Preferably, a leveraged weight of value makes your offer a bargain or a no-brainer.

"The successful people I know aren't obsessed with beating out the other person and stepping on others' heads to get to the top. Their motivation, instead, is to do such a good job at their assigned task that they come to be regarded as first in a fast field of excellent talent."
—— **Don Seibert**
Former CEO of J.C. Penney

Your Leverage Position Is an Equation:

A *Sales*Mind constantly asks, "What is my leverage position (strength or weakness) in this transaction as I interact with the buyer for a decision?" This question is vital because the goal is to have positive leverage, or pull on your side, with the buyer (but never manipulation). The business of sales calls for drawing your buyers toward the sale with their own desire, not pushing them with your agenda. I call this dynamic interaction "the persuasion equation" because the strength of one variable is equal to the strength of the next three:

The degree of your **Leverage** (present position) with your buyer is equal to the sum of:

- The degree of **Connection** they have with you (Chapter 5)...
- Plus the degree of **Value** they perceive about your product or service (Chapter 6)...
- Plus the degree of **Urgency** they possess to decide now (Chapter 7).

Note that all three occur simultaneously.

This total relationship is the basis from which *Sales*Minds sense whether or not they are positioned to earn their buyer's business—and at what price. Let me offer a global example of how the "persuasion equation" worked:

In the 1980s, President Ronald Reagan used positive leverage to break the back of the Soviet Union and win the Cold War. He didn't do it with words. He didn't do it with hopes. He didn't do it with inaction (as did the Carter administration). He did it with *leverage*. He led America's no-compromise position of victory. He called it "peace through strength."

- **Connection**. The president was open and honest with the American people about what type of danger we faced from the Soviets. He was straightforward enough to call them "the evil empire." He connected with us, and the vast majority of us *trusted* him.

- **Value**. He was clear about the intense Soviet threat to our national interest for generations to come. He discussed directly with the American people the high degree of personal value of winning this war for our children and grandchildren.

- **Urgency**. Our Commander-in-Chief compelled us to deal with this adversary *now*, and called upon Congress to immediately start funding the Strategic Defense Initiative ("Star Wars"). Also, history will never forget how he urgently challenged President Gorbachev on worldwide TV with the immortal words, "Mr. Gorbachev, tear down this wall."

Together, those dynamics generated (on the Soviets) an enormous degree of:

- **Leverage**. In the minds of the American people (and most of the world), it was the high degree of Reagan's connection on the issue, plus the clear perception of value of the mission's success, plus the urgency of the victory, that together generated the leverage position for America to fully persuade the Soviets to not only abandon their expansionist objectives, but also to abandon Communism.

Soon after, the Soviet Union imploded after seventy dreadful years (Amazingly, the nation that emerged, Russia, is now slowly moving to become our ally, although many sticking points remain.) It wasn't peace through hope for Dutch Reagan. It was peace through *strength*.

Leverage Involves Competing Economic Motives

To fully understand leverage in business, one must also understand the inherent supply/demand struggle between the buyer and seller, which is their "economic tug of war." This tug should be expected even in the closest business relationships because the buyer and seller have one key set of opposite motives:

Buyer. Buyers always want to receive the greatest possible value at the lowest possible price.

Seller. Sellers always want to receive as much money as possible while giving up the least amount of cost possible.

There's nothing wrong with these motives. The only thing wrong is when the seller doesn't realize what's going on. Buyers always understand because it is their money, and that could give them a transactional advantage.

A SalesMind influences buyer connection, value, and urgency, recognizing both parties will position each other for the money paid in a transaction.

CUMULATIVE LEVERAGE

Cumulative leverage is the total impact on all of your buyers from all leverage variables in your business. It's your total business position comprised of the following elements:

- **Cooperation Leverage.** The total degree of cooperation exerted by everyone in your organization toward satisfying all of your buyers.

- **Quality Leverage.** The connection, value, and urgency experienced in one buyer.

- **Quantity Leverage.** The entire amount of buyers being leveraged at any one time.

- **Price Leverage.** The positioning of price in relation to buyer desire and the competition.

- **Transaction Leverage.** The seller's persuasion skill in a negotiation.

You can be certain that your total position will affect your buyers' total perception.

Cumulative Leverage Has Two Buyer Effects

On the heart: Emotional leverage (trust) can create enough financial leverage to transact.

On the mind: Financial leverage—unquestionable business value—operating in reverse, can also create enough emotional leverage to transact.

To bring the most powerful combination possible to bear on making the sale, create a strong mix of both emotional and financial leverage. Leverage is perceived before the sale and also evaluated constantly after the sale by both parties. Remember, there is a strong desire by both buyer and seller for a leveraged position in the business relationship.

*A Sales**Mind** leverages every possible buyer benefit to maximize profitable selling prices.*

COOPERATION LEVERAGE

*Sales*Minds cooperate with managers, service people, technicians, office staff, administrators, and any other employees for maximum team impact on the buyer. You will never hear a *Sales*Mind say, "Yeah, they blew it again in the warehouse." That is not the attitude of cooperation. Why blame someone else?

Help fix the problem. Be a solution-creator, not a problem-multiplier.

Cooperation and synergy are valuable resources. In reverse, isn't friction between departments a potential killer in achieving higher sales?

You also never know when your boss or someone else on your team has the opportunity to apply leverage or positive influence that can sway the buyer to purchase. It could be a free influence for you.

Cooperation Leverage Requires Partners:

1. **Alignment with the marketing department's influence.** The *Sales*Mind has to understand what their company's products and services *are* and what they *will do* for the buyer. The marketing and sales messages must then match in their delivery.

   Make every attempt to influence the marketing department to consider and respond to the buyer's needs at the field level. Sometimes the sales force is the very best tool for marketing research. Marketing today is like guerrilla warfare, and is not effective when implemented as an ivory-tower approach from the home office.

2. **Harmony with all other departments.** The *Sales*Mind is a critical player in terms of team selling. Think about any great team. They create a great performance through the harmony of goals, emotions, talents, and attitudes. Don't you want to be an integral part of your company's team that moves forward, responds, and outperforms buyer expectations?

> *"Therefore encourage one another and build up each other, just as in fact you are doing."*
> —— **I Thessalonians 5:11**

Are You a Leader?

*Sales*Minds are leaders. They don't wait for others to cooperate in team leverage. They take action first by:

- Walking their own talk and setting an example for attitude and behavior.
- Understanding potential frictions and working to eliminate communication barriers between Sales and Service, Management and Sales, Office and Warehouse, etc.
- Desiring to help internally and be a servant leader.
- Communicating with urgency and consistency.
- Jumping into situations that will foster respect and set service examples.
- Adjusting when necessary, being honest, and bonding with others. People always bond in intense common action. Consider the bond soldiers have in warfare.

- Reinforcing their role in the team context.
- Connecting with all levels of their own company's management.

*A Sales**Mind** is happy to harmonize with every company employee to maximize transaction position. Not doing so is just plain stupid.*

FOR QUALITY LEVERAGE, "GO DEEP"

Do you build buyer relationships that are "deep" regardless of circumstances? Quality leverage is simply the degree of strength of the seller's position in the buyer's mind when considering a transaction. Because that position is also closely related to what the buyer will pay, the seller wants that relationship to be very deeply rooted in the buyer's mind.

"Your financial requirements or wants have nothing whatsoever to do with your worth. Your value is established entirely by your ability to render useful service or your capacity to influence others to render such service."
—— **Napoleon Hill**
Think and Grow Rich

There are three progressive states of quality leverage between the buyer and the seller:

- The buyer's beginning perception of you at first contact.
- The current moment of your interaction.
- The desired effect of the seller just before the transaction.

Beginning Leverage

Buyer and seller leverage always has a *beginning* position of some degree. Leveraging begins the minute the buyer becomes aware of the seller or their product. That awareness can also exist before there is personal contact. If you were to examine the quality of beginning leverage of every sales scenario, you would find one of the four levels below:

1. **Absolute Best.** You were referred to a potential buyer with a need, and they immediately called you. They can be closed quickly at a great price because there is great beginning leverage. Close them now at maximum price when they call.

2. **Second Best.** You became aware that you were referred to a potential buyer but you were the one who made the first call. They still can be closed at a good price. Leverage is slightly down, but still good. You simply have to deduct points because you had to call.

3. **OK.** A potential buyer saw an ad or mailer and called in, but keep in mind, they are probably shopping. The sale can be closed with work and a differentiation in value from your competition. You have to develop this relationship from the moment you connect.

4. **Takes Work.** You made the initial contact and initiated all the elements of the potential sale. All sales steps are necessary. Just be a *Sales*Mind.

Remember, when a buyer and seller meet, there is always a state of beginning leverage position that the *Sales*Mind must maximize to move toward a profitable transaction.

Current Leverage

From beginning leverage to now, you will have advanced an account or single sale to a position of leverage at this moment, or your *current* leverage with that account.

The following grid is a very powerful tool to score the quality of your current leverage in an account. Let's say you scored one of your own top accounts like this:

Current Leverage Per Sale/Account

Possible Levers of Business
Value With My/Our Buyer   *Quality Now**

> * Key to Ratings: Low 1 or 2; Medium 3 or 4; High 5 or 6.

1.	Current Relationship	4
2.	Uniqueness in Market	2
3.	Niche in Market	2
4.	Inventory Availability	4
5.	My Personal Impact	5
6.	Added Value Specifics	5
7.	Meeting, Fiscal, or Holiday Urgencies	3
8.	Testimonials or Statistics	6
9.	Service Record	5
10.	Market Share or Industry Position	3
11.	Pricing Advantages	2
12.	Line of Credit Strength	1
13.	Marketing Support	4
14.	Co-Op Dollars Offered	2
15.	Decision-Maker Connection	6
16.	Creation of Desire Evident in Sale	4
17.	Volume vs. Margin Pricing	2
18.	Staff Relationships with Buyer	5
19.	Your Personal Financial Strength	6
20.	Company's Financial Strength	5

Total...76

AVERAGE SCORE (TOTAL 76 DIVIDED BY 20) = 3.8

What was the basis for your score of each value lever?

What is the meaning of your cumulative (76) and average (3.8) scores?

Which levers are most important in this account or sale?

What specific actions should you take now to move each important lever to a higher number?

Can you think of other important value levers to add to my list of 20?

How would you benefit if you did this exercise with each sale or account?

Desired Leverage

Key: Your goal is to take this current assessment and advance the score of each important lever to its *desired* position so as to accomplish the transaction at a profitable price. In other words, you want to take sales actions that *will add to the value of each appropriate lever in the buyer's mind.* Don't hesitate, because I guarantee that your buyer is trying to advance their buying position with you (to get more from you and get your price down).

*A Sales**Mind** drives every buyer benefit to its deepest level in the relationship to maximize transaction position.*

FOR QUANTITY LEVERAGE, "GO WIDE"

We know that quality or deep leverage is a per-sale or per-account factor with buyers. On the other hand, leverage *quantity* is the total amount of buyers the seller is leveraging at any one time. It's "wide" leverage, and here are a few benefits:

- It gives you enough buyers to eliminate needing any one particular sale or account at all.
- It rewards your total business by exerting positive decision leverage on every individual buyer relationship.
- It creates courage to command a high price per-sale. We will cover these dynamics in greater detail in Chapter 11, Coverage.

Quantity leverage results from having adequate coverage (contact activity) to fill your pipeline with the right kind of buyers—to do this you must go wide. Understanding the following relationships between leverage and price is vital:

1. **Low leverage generates low price.** With a small buyer universe resulting from low coverage, you will consistently have low emotional and financial leverage. The result is a consistently low price at transaction. You need each buyer too much in order to survive.

2. **High leverage generates high price.** With a large buyer universe resulting from high coverage, you will consistently have high emotional and financial leverage. The result is a consistently high price at transaction. You don't have to sell any one buyer to succeed.

Please take this oath today to always enjoy the impact of quantity leverage: "I will prospect daily, network, database, tradeshow, advertise, promote, follow-up, and market my program to enjoy the highest possible emotional and financial leverage that results from going wide."

The Final Leverage Equation

We now have established the fundamental relationships of buyer/seller leverage. If those relationships were stated as an equation, it might look like this:

$$QLeb \ \times \ QLab = CLyb = Success$$

Spelled out, this equation reads as follows: The quality of leverage of each buyer **(QLeb)** multiplied by the quantity of leverage of all buyers **(QLab)** equals the cumulative leverage of your business **(CLyb)**, which in turn, equals **success**.

*Sales*Minds *must generate leverage in each transaction multiplied by many transactions to attain maximum leverage for their business.*

PRICE LEVERAGE

Price in a transaction is directly related to the degree of leverage between the buyer and the seller. In supply/demand terms, a low price is achieved when supply of the seller exceeds demand of the buyer. In reverse, a high price is achieved when seller supply is less than buyer demand.

Buying an airline ticket provides a clear example of these dynamics. Let's say you need to make an immediate buying decision two days out from a flight date because of an unplanned, but necessary business trip. You will pay a very large premium. Why? Because your immediate need to fly is price leverage for the airline. However, if you can plan a trip two months out, you can practically fly for free (price leverage for you).

You can even go online day by day and watch a ticket price increase as you get closer to its flight date. If one carrier dominates that route, you pay even more. The good news today is that with online purchasing and extreme competition in the airline industry, you can probably still get a pretty good deal. Airlines though, with frequent flyer programs and incentives, still try to leverage your loyalty and keep prices up. Airline ticket purchase clearly demonstrates the general laws of price leverage as dictated by supply and demand.

With those price principles in mind, let's refocus on a sales relationship and remember this absolute key in a buying decision: The combination of quality and quantity leverage will offer the *Sales*Mind a confident sense of the price a buyer will pay in single or multiple transactions. Having a sense of price leverage *just prior* to a decision is particularly useful, important, and valuable.

Pre-Decision Price Leverage (PDPL)

Just prior to every decision (good or bad), there is a state of leverage that exists between a *Sales*Mind and a buyer. I call this condition "Pre-Decision Price Leverage," or **PDPL**. There are two conditions of **PDPL**:

1. **The PDPL is known before the closing appointment or call.** This condition allows you to still influence, send things, and handle objections. You can boost value in one last chance before negotiating price in person. You can prepare to negotiate, a big advantage for you to obtain your price.

2. **The PDPL is not known before the closing appointment or call.** This condition does not allow for you to provide extra influence or handle objections prior to the closing meeting to boost value. You find out your program's value and respond accordingly as you negotiate price in person. This is the moment of truth for your skills to obtain your price.

Whether known before a decision or not, a *Sales*Mind always keeps a tight focus on **PDPL**.

Leverage Your Price Results

Of course, every negotiation and transaction will yield some price for the seller. You will basically have one of three price results after a buyer's decision:

1. **"Blue-Chip" Leverage (highest price).** You secure the best price possible. This leverage normally exists in scenarios with very unique products, powerful companies, high-profile individuals, call-in business, superior individual confidence at presentation, and qualified referrals. The seller is much stronger and more valuable in negotiation than is the buyer's position to want to resist. Remember Wal-Mart?

   There is also Rush:

   - Heard on over 600 stations by 22 million listeners per week.
   - Commands the noon to three o'clock time slot in AM radio.
   - Spawned the growth of the news/talk format from 300 to 1400 stations in 12 years.
   - Caused radio ratings and revenues to soar in conservative talk radio.
   - Was fired from seven previous radio jobs.
   - Earned an 8-year, 285 million dollar contract in 2001.

   —— Rush Limbaugh "Blue Chip" factoids

2. "Just Above The Pack" Leverage (medium-high price). You are perceived to have a small competitive advantage, meaning that you need to close the transaction now while your position is strongest.

3. "Arbitrary" (lack of) Leverage (medium-low price). You are perceived as equal to other vendors and will be in a price war to close. Your product or service is perceived as a commodity. *Sales*Minds—together with their products—are *never* perceived as a commodity.

Price achieved in a transaction is closely related to the seller's ability and willingness to walk away and go to another buyer.

TRANSACTION LEVERAGE

Dr. Chester L. Karrass, the late author of several books on negotiation strategies, was a ground-breaker. His work is being carried on by his son, Gary, who wrote: *Negotiate to Close: How to Make More Successful Deals.*

"Power is what you think it is. Those who think they have no power negotiate poorly and weakly—even if they do have power. Those who think they have power negotiate from strength—even if they really don't have power."
—— **Gary Karrass**

From Position to Paycheck

The *Sales*Mind successfully orchestrates sales events towards their finality: The moment when the money is exchanged. It's not just closing, nor is it just a decision. It's the diligence to make sure the decision becomes a profitable transaction. The decision though, is the moment of truth. It's a magical moment when the validity of your sales claims matches the buyer's belief in you. That moment is signified by a desire to transact.

Do You Have Command of the Five Key Negotiation Dynamics?

The first key is the ability to talk money comfortably. Do you calmly and precisely write down dollar figures? Do you have control of your calculations and math steps? Do you talk fluidly and openly about dollars?

The second key is understanding your transaction's timing. What do you know about the buyer's budget, time of year for buying, and release procedures?

The third key is possessing knowledge of competitive activity and position. Do you know everything possible about the performance and involvement of current suppliers and competitive bidders? You should also have—but use wisely—what I call a "walk-away cost." That is a final discount you may choose to offer a buyer. That final discount should be equal to your continued sales cost of pursuing them and with the assumption that they will buy from your competitor.

The fourth key is understanding the dynamics of cash, time on money, and opportunity cost. This is not an economics course. But if these terms don't ring a bell, you need to learn them.

The fifth key is being prepared to meet objections based on the process of investment judgment and risk. Buyers assume a risk when they invest in your product or service. Can you explain exactly why you are the best possible investment and worthy of their money?

You might consider that negotiating these dynamics is complicated. They can be as complex as or simple as you choose except that you have to match their complexity to your type of business. But I assure you, the deeper you apply these negotiation dynamics in selling anything, the more income you will earn.

To simplify the use of these variables, here are some questions to help you define how you can more successfully and profitably negotiate:

- **Decision-maker.** I know this is obvious, but are you talking directly with the individual(s) who can approve or veto a transaction? If not, do that first.

- **Position.** This is the platform of this chapter. Position is the respective bargaining strength for both the buyer and the seller. What elements of specific value do you bring in relation to the needs, competitive choices, and urgency of the buyer?

- **Objective.** Are the positions and desired outcomes of the seller and buyer clearly defined? Obviously, from your view, you should ask and determine these buyer objectives.

- **Time.** Is time (urgency) a decision variable for the buyer to transact?

- **Information.** Do you have a complete purchasing and service history, competitive proposal loss count, and personal profile of your buyer?

- **Elements.** When you have discovered the variables in a negotiation, do you separate each one and slow down until each variable is individually agreed to before moving on? If so, you will protect a higher price.

- **Service.** Are you aware and have documentation of a buyer's service history and your service reputation, especially if this is a first time buyer?

- **Words.** Can you articulate the specific elements of your value to the buyer with compelling smoothness?

- **Responses.** Are you totally prepared to handle the objections and questions that will come your way from the buyer on both your program and the money?

- **Evidence.** Do you have a varied and compelling number of testimonial letters, statistics, and positive surveys to objectively support your value position?

If not, it's all claims, and those claims may be doubted.

- **Goodies.** Can you save something to toss in at the last minute as a value-add to clinch the deal and be a hero?

- **Relationship.** Do you have the all-time best negotiating variable working in your favor? It is a positive, honest, and contributing relationship with the buyer. Nothing replaces trust.

My position with you is plain and simple. You need to answer these questions *before* you enter into a negotiation with the buyer. If you can answer them successfully, you will close more sales at higher prices and have a greater command of the sequence of the transaction.

The Transaction Sequence

We have now defined the elements of a successful transaction. Let's place them in a sequence from one to three. The transaction sequence may proceed with agonizing slowness—or it may move quickly. However, it always involves all three phases, no matter how slowly or quickly they proceed. In a successful selling sequence, a *Sales*Mind establishes position, negotiates, and then creates a transaction as they:

1. Position for Negotiation
2. Negotiate for Highest Price X
3. Transact at Highest Price X

Position Components Details

Connection Quality?
Long-Term Contract?
Short-Term Contract?
Add-ons or Supplies?
Purchase Agreement?
Add to Account Balance?
Connection Quality?
Personal-Life Value?
Urgencies?
Information?
Decision-Maker?
Credibility?
Uniqueness?
Team Cooperation?
Coverage of All Accounts?
Marketing Support?
Competitive Strength?

Negotiation

Terms (time/s)?
Interest Rate?
Volume and Margins?
Lease?
Future Price Increases?
Shipping Included?
Training Included?
Service Guarantees?
Support Guarantees?
Liabilities Incurred?
Legalities Incurred?
Length of Contract?
Guaranteed Renewal?

Transaction Details

Deposit Check?
Purchase Order Number?
Credit Application?
Purchase Agreement?
Wire Transaction?

Goal: Highest Price X_____

*A Sales**Mind** manages a sale from position to
negotiation, resulting in a transaction for money.*

Leverage is the *price* of persuasion. Your charge is
to take all of the persuasive power of your connection,
value, urgency, and leverage positions and synchronize
their impact with buyers. In doing so, you have positioned
almost all your knowledge and skill toward maximizing
your selling reputation and income. I said almost—there's
one more issue to master, and you never have enough of it.

PART III: TIMING

LEVERAGING TIME

T ime. We all want more of it and greater satisfaction from it. *Money* magazine surveyed households with incomes of $75,000, asking whether they would rather have more time or more money.

"More time," 57% said, while only 40% wanted more money.

We also want successful results. *Sales*Minds know how to achieve those results within the limited time available to them. They know that outcome involves effective timing.

But when do you have effective timing?

The answer: *by having a successful relationship with time as it relates to maximizing opportunities.* You must have a successful relationship position with time. To acquire that position, your yield from time must out-leverage your waste of time.

Timing is an action taken at a specific time and directed at the best possible opportunity. *Sales*Minds fulfill plans, carry out decisions, and take actions that operate in harmony to maximize their results. They are consistently at the right place with the right idea for the right person—all at the right time.

THE MISSION OF THE NEXT FOUR CHAPTERS IS TO HELP YOU ESTABLISH A POSITIVE RELATIONSHIP POSITION WITH TIME.

In a time-sensitive pursuit of that goal, the SalesMind answers these interlocking questions about timing:

- **Priority (Chapter 9) What is the *object* of my timing?**

- **Control (Chapter 10) What creates the *flow* of my timing?**

- **Coverage (Chapter 11) What is the *scope* of my timing?**

- **Adjustment (Chapter 12) How do I *change* my timing?**

Leveraging time takes daily effort. It takes energy. But are you leveraging the one resource you can't buy back? That resource is *time*. The answer begins with how you plan your daily and weekly actions.

PRIORITY

SOMEDAY YOU WILL DIE

Separtember 11. I was finishing up some morning business before flying that day to Florida for a seminar when my wife Demetri called with the shocking news that terrorism had struck our country.

Everyone remembers where they were and what they were doing when the hijacked planes full of people slammed into the World Trade Center, the Pentagon, and rural Pennsylvania. We all remember how we felt after rushing to a TV to see what was happening and being greeted by gruesome images and shocking words.

Normality died that morning. The most important priorities in life crossed everyone's mind. In an instant, we all knew things in the United States were now different.

Our national priorities had changed in a flash. Only ten months before the tragic day—in the twilight of our carefree days—a controversial presidential election had gripped the nation's attention. Its aftermath was arguably the most bitter since Abraham Lincoln's election ignited the Civil War more than a century earlier.

In those otherwise tranquil times before 9/11, the political parties in this country argued about Social Security, taxes, and prescription drugs. As always, both parties were scrambling for position on issues that had traction as priorities in the public mind.

Nothing had traction after 9/11 except our country's response to these terrorist killers. Our first and most important priority was instantly defined for us in one catastrophic morning, a few hours that, like Pearl Harbor, will live forever in infamy.

PRIORITY IS THE OBJECT OF YOUR TIMING

Priority is defined as "taking precedence in importance or value, or to arrange in order of importance." Accomplishing goals by establishing priorities is crucial to success. The problem in accomplishing goals is always limited time. A *Sales*Mind never has enough time in a day. Not to do everything. They have to make the best possible choices in time use. In the multitude of seminars I've done over the years, the number one issue of a *Sales*Mind at any experience level is "not enough time to get things done to meet sales goals." That reminds me of the coach that once said, "We could win every game if we only had more time."

The good news here is at least every *Sales*Mind is aware of that. The bad news is this: that reality will never change. There is never enough total time for all tasks. You have to choose what will deliver the most impact. It is not enough just to do things. You have to define the best things to do first. Then, you have to do those things well.

> "**Industry.** *Lose no time. Be always employed in something useful. Cut off all unnecessary actions.*"
> —— **Benjamin Franklin**
> Number 6 of his 13 Virtues

PRIORITY BY PRINCIPLE

It is vital to absorb and apply these principles to help you establish and execute priorities:

Do the most productive and profitable sales activities first, prior to anything else. Let everything else wait. That standard involves decisions, choices, and a system for action.

Resist doing the urgent. Everything will scream its urgency, but everything will not provide an equal return on your investment of time.

Identify those accounts and activities that present the highest opportunities for revenue and profit, considering your own resources. In doing so, you have placed yourself in the best possible position to leverage timing within your best opportunities.

Every *Sales*Mind faces the same daily dilemma involving time. Remembering this reality may make it a bit easier to deal with your own difficulties in sorting out what action will deliver the greatest return on any given day.

The time dilemma begins with this reality: there are just too many things or tasks to do. Let's say you have a lot more things to do than available time to do them. The reality is that your tasks and time don't and never will equalize, thus the need to prioritize your list daily.

Have in writing a pre-determined daily set of the most productive things to do that day. Then make decisions that discern and implement actions in line with those priorities.

Every *Sales*Mind should have the goal of producing the most sales possible within the limited time available. Without that objective, the average salesperson drifts along doing the things that scream the loudest or are the easiest and most pleasant to do. Whether or not those actions are productive of sales is left to chance, which means that few of them will be the most productive use of time.

Do not be connected to the wrong (unprofitable) things. The *Sales*Mind also reacts to the truth that it is not that you worked today, but what you worked *on* today that matters. Time cannot be wasted on the unproductive. I'm not talking about non-business thoughts or activities that renew and refresh. I am talking about just "putting in time" and trying to excuse non-productivity.

As we'll discuss in Chapters 10 and 11, information control and territory coverage help reveal the most profitable sales opportunities. On the flip side, effective control and coverage also lower the risk of choosing the wrong opportunities that reduce profitable returns.

Priorities involve assumptions and decisions. Good decisions based on good assumptions equal good results. Bad decisions based on bad assumptions equal bad results.

Get rid of the thought and statement, "I don't have enough time" because you might believe it. Focus rather on believing you have a system of discipline to produce the most with the time you have. A *Sales*Mind never feels time helplessness.

Within limited time, a SalesMind establishes priorities to maximize opportunities.

INVEST IN THE CONSTITUTION

That's the constitution of a priority, or what a priority is *based on*. Constitute means "to make up or be the components or elements of." A priority should always be made up of predetermined objectives and guidelines for use of time and energy.

Consider the Constitution of the United States. For over two hundred years, this document of principles, rights, and laws has maintained the most successful and longest lasting form of government in the world.

The framers considered many ideas, systems of government, rules of law, and human desires for freedom to arrive at the final document. Priorities were established. As a system of priorities, the Constitution was constructed as a careful framework of elements for freedom and government. The return on the time invested in setting those priorities has never been approached in value.

*Sales*Minds also have endless tasks and demands on their limited time from which they seek to extract the best possible sales results. They too have to set priorities to serve as a careful framework based on the most important elements to operate their business.

One key principle for your priority system: It is not the *setting* of priorities that is the (only) key. It is the *return on an investment* of prioritized tasks that matters most. You must have the proper and most productive tasks prioritized, and then you will achieve the highest results.

Sales priorities have an effective basis when they result in actions that create the highest possible buyer satisfaction and loyalty from the best possible buyers. Properly and effectively used, they:

- Result in maximum profits for you and your company.
- Support your personal values, goals, and emotional life.
- Reflect harmony between short-term and long-term priorities.
- Are written as action-plans.
- Are fulfilled as daily, weekly, monthly, quarterly, and annual actions.

- Are assisted by tools to organize, measure, and achieve.
- Assist others on your company team to better serve high-revenue buyers.

"Be very careful, then, how you live—not as unwise but as wise, making the most of every opportunity."
—— **Ephesians 5:16**

Remember, the maximum effect of a priority comes from not just having them, but rather from what they are based on, and from acting on them.

DO YOU EXPECT TO GET A RETURN ON YOUR INVESTMENT?

*Sales*Minds are focused on a return on the investment of time, knowledge, and energy. Therefore they have expectations for setting priorities. Those expectations are:

1. **Highest return on investment (ROI) possible from all activities.** You invest in decisions and actions for a return. You will also discover in reverse that as you assess the potential and sales probability of an account or activity further, a return may not be there and that item needs to be reduced in priority. If the return is simply not there now, an alternate account or activity is the better selection. You must validate and analyze the return on your priorities continuously.

2.   **Highest ROI from customers.** You help and invest in customers for a return. Customers spend money with you, and they have ongoing buying decisions with you. What specifically are your priorities with these buyers?

- To gain stronger relationships with decision-makers?
- To gain better relationships with influencers?
- To pursue more account revenue or gross profit per transaction?
- To add new lines?
- To extend new or better value-added components?
- To handle problems or make service calls?
- To gather more information on their business or personal information on key people?
- To confirm your company is providing service and value above their expectations?
- To sincerely help people?

3.   **Highest ROI from prospects.** You invest in prospects for a return. Prospects have not spent money with you yet. What specifically are your priorities with these buyers?

- To connect with decision-makers and other staff?
- To gain some general profile information on the landscape of their business?
- To qualify their business potential?
- To determine who their current supplier is and on what scale?
- To assess the probability that you could propose and close a first piece of business?

- To discover if they have problems you can solve?
- To compare their volume and margin potential to your current buyers?
- To survey for information?

Two additional categories within the business framework will also have some priority time allocated to them:

4. **Highest ROI from company activities.** You invest in your company for a return. There are always established company requirements for your time. What specifically are your priorities for these demands?

- To gain new knowledge from a training meeting?
- To learn about the future and vision of the company from key executives?
- To fashion more efficient methods for collecting and reporting information?
- To build rapport with employees in other departments?
- To learn ways to reduce wasted time and to lower sales cost?
- To absorb new product updates and their value to buyers?
- To create better ways to communicate within the entire company team?
- To learn about internal company investments, 401K, insurance or stock issues, product or service problems?
- To brown-nose the boss? Just kidding. (I think).

5. **Highest ROI from business or personal enrichment.** You invest in personal learning for a return. *Sales*Minds are constantly advancing their current skills or gaining new ones. What specifically are your priorities for personal learning?

    • To assess how much time and energy would be involved to learn new skills?
    • To review new content for its usefulness in your sales or personal life?
    • To upgrade your technical skills to compete at the highest level in your market?
    • To prepare yourself for management?
    • To reestablish strong sales skill fundamentals?
    • To renew good study habits?

*Sales***Minds** *base their priorities on predetermined rules, expectations, and return on investment of their resources.*

ROADBLOCKS TO EFFECTIVE PRIORITIES

What about when your priorities are either not in place or just don't seem to be working in producing results? Review the possible causes below:

Laziness. You must find the discipline and energy to identify which buyers, decisions, and actions are the most profitable to pursue. If you don't, you will not be a *Sales*Mind, period!

Lack of analysis in planning. Your priorities and plans have to involve evaluation of your strategy, training, and resources. Have you planned your work and worked your plan? Without thinking and diligence, that futile old non-plan called "winging it" will control your actions.

Responding to the urgent, not the important. Urgent means it feels important now. Everything in business, including the agendas of buyers, managers, associates, and suppliers, feels important. Other people motivate you in that direction. You have to decide what is important and has a yield—for you.

Interruptions. Everyone has interruptions. In business though, a *Sales*Mind has to adopt and communicate clear rules with fairness and reciprocity with those involved in their business. Respond to people as though you have rules that govern the conditions in which people can randomly take your time. For example:

- Did those people get their own information straight before coming to you?
- Did they first try to solve the problem on their own before calling you?
- What level of buyer desires your time?
- Could they have left you a simple email so that you wouldn't have to make notes?

Rules won't stop interruptions. However—if written down, made known to others, and enforced—rules and requirements will minimize interruptions, and make others more accountable before breaking into your time.

Not saying "no." In the appropriate scenario and with the appropriate person, can you say "no" to a request for your time? Yes. If you can't, you have major problems that will grow worse over time. It is not possible to do everything for everybody. You have to make time choices based on reality. Some people look for someone who can't say "no" and dump all their work on them. Watch out for these folks and protect yourself.

Stress. It is a fact that if you are under major stress, your priorities will become dim, disorganized, and ineffective. You will find yourself again doing the perceived urgent items—generally urgent to someone else—instead of the things that realistically are important to your ability to maximize your income. Your productivity and profitability then will be reduced and the stress will increase.

Be sure to exercise, get enough sleep, eat right, keep your personal and business priorities in writing, and review them at least once a day. Make adjustments by degree if necessary. Too much stress fogs up a good plan.

Not factoring in "flex" time. One of the worst mistakes you can make as a SalesMind is to plan 100% of the time in your day. That's right. Here's the reason. Let's say that if interruptions carve out 20% of your day, you now have to do 120% each day. That's impossible. Plan 80% of your day and leave the rest for unknowns. Don't worry. The time will fill in.

Sales*Minds *know their priorities can be sabotaged and make their timing ineffective—so they figure in daily flex time.

HOW DO PRIORITIES HELP GENERATE PROFITABLE RESULTS?

Priorities help you generate maximum sales results—that's their purpose. Specifically, they help clarify revenue sources, drive selling decisions, and crystallize action-plans:

Priorities Help Clarify Revenue Sources

After setting some general goals and guidelines for your priorities, it's important to examine where the profitable sales dollars are to support those goals. You now have the job to clarify, forecast, and target revenue sources. There are only two groups that sales dollars come from:

Customers (paying now)

Prospects (not paying yet)

Your job is to accumulate historical data on your sales territory/account base and then generate a forecast. The data needs to be driven by the following questions for an accurate forecast:

How much customer revenue contributes to your forecast? What is their percentage contribution to your forecast? Who and where are these customers?

How much prospect revenue contributes to your forecast? What is their percentage contribution to your forecast? Who and where are these prospects?

Priorities Help Drive Selling Decisions

*Sales*Minds make scores of decisions every day to follow through on their priorities. In taking specific and effective actions, *Sales*Minds constantly ask these "Questions of Decision" (using them as filters) to focus their actions:

- How much daily flextime should I plan for contingencies?
- What specific sales call or account elements do I need to plan?
- Who should I contact in the account for the most impact?
- When should I call a contact for the best chance of connection?
- What is the return on investment in each call?
- How do I align the highest level of effort with the most important activities?

Priorities Help Crystallize Action

Here is where the priority rubber meets the road. If you have not been paying attention to this chapter, pay attention now. *Sales*Minds turn their written priorities into written action plans. Action planning means focusing on what to do now. An effective action plan will define first actions to get started as well as sustaining actions to keep going. Be sure to go back to Chapter 3, Action, and review those elements.

Based on goals/forecasts, validated assumptions, and collected data, a *Sales*Mind produces intelligent business development priorities. Those identified (written) priorities will carry the greatest possible return of profitable sales with the least risk of misdirected time.

This is a sample format of how your prioritized four--part Action Plan should look:

ACTION PLAN

1. Priority (Specific) Customers to Grow Revenue:

Target 1:_____

Target 2:_____

Target 3:_____

First Actions to be taken now:

_____

_____
.

Sustaining Actions to be taken:

_____

2. Priority (Specific) Prospects to Target for Appointments and Presentations:

Target 1:_____

Target 2:_____

Target 3:_____

First Actions to be taken now:

_____

_____

Sustaining Actions to be taken:

_____

_____

3. Priority (Specific) Activities of Your Company for Service or Education:

Activity 1:_____

Activity 2:_____

Activity 3:_____

First Actions (required or) to be taken:

_____

Sustaining Actions to be taken:

---

4. Priority (Specific) Business or Personal Enrichment Projects:

Project 1:_____

Project 2:_____

Project 3:_____

First Actions to be taken:

Sustaining Actions to be taken:

---

*A Sales**Mind** uses information, decisions, and action plans to maximize their most profitable priorities.*

Priority is the *object* of timing. It answers the question, "What is important that I am trying to have effective timing with?" But did you know that the objects of your timing have ingredients that you have to collect and control? Wait until you see how every successful modern day *Sales*Mind—and business—leverage every second to earn the big bucks.

10

CONTROL

WHY CREDIT CARD COMPANIES ARE RICH

D o you use credit cards? I thought so. Most credit card companies, being run by big banks, operate strictly within a set of rules for maximum timing of their business opportunities. Those rules make them highly successful. Once you are caught up in these rules, they can be upsetting and drive you deep into debt. Information *control* is what enables these rules to work:

- **Profit.** The goal of these selling companies is profit for their investors, period.

- **Time.** They have to produce that profit within a limited amount of time, which may be their monthly or quarterly earnings periods. Therefore they have to focus on which demographic groups will produce that profit.

   With this purpose, they target groups who have immediate and highly emotional spending desires. Those desires will make the timing of the credit card marketing and response (and the subsequent spending by the cardholders, which is the purpose of the exercise) successful.

- **Priority.** Entry-level college students are one of those prime groups, or in other words, a marketing priority for the company.

   Experience tells these companies that college freshmen are prime targets because, in their first time away from home, they want freedom and purchasing power (even though many of them can't handle the finances). An added long-term bonus is that they can acquire lots of lifelong customers this way.

   The timing of marketing to these eager freshmen is the key element of the credit card demand. The companies also know that because of limited income, the students tend to make only the minimum payment, the most profitable scenario for the company.

- **Information.** So every year within this priority category, the companies purchase enrollment information from colleges, set up booths at athletic and orientation events, and even share the lucrative profits from the credit cards with the colleges.

By the end of this decade, the 300 largest U.S. universities will be getting nearly one billion dollars every year from the banking industry.

- **Knowledge.** These marketing activities are based on profitable knowledge of proven behavior. This is the knowledge base:

  ❏ Ninety-two percent of students carry at least one credit card by their sophomore year.
  ❏ Twenty-one percent are carrying balances between $3,000 and $7,000.
  ❏ Students double their average credit card debt and triple the number of cards in their wallets between the time they arrive on campus and graduation.
  ❏ Default levels are even manageable because the companies know that many parents will bail their kids out by paying the bills.

- **Power.** It all began with specific information. This student enrollment information control is financial power, and that power leverages into high profits.

I don't fully agree with this type of marketing, but it dramatically emphasizes how the relationship of information control and market timing operate to produce profits.

INFORMATION CONTROL IS THE FLOW OF TIMING

Control is defined as "to exercise authority or influence over or to regulate, direct, or dominate." When I consider that definition, I think of the role of blood flow and the circulatory system in nourishing the systems of the body. A body cannot function without the flow of blood, and a *Sales*Mind's business cannot function without a healthy flow of information to nourish his or her business.

An information system carries information from buyers, the market, and the competition to the *Sales*Mind. That information alerts the *Sales*Mind as to how, why, when, where, and with whom to execute selling and service activities that will produce transactions. A *Sales*Mind has to be able to access and use information today to have control of their business.

A *Sales*Mind uses information to take priority actions that have maximum impact with the buyer. Those actions may be closing a sale, presenting a new product line, asking for referrals, or calling for a key appointment. Information is the map and the compass that places a *Sales*Mind in a consistent position to have effective timing with their buyers. You can't establish priorities without information. Information is the DNA of a priority.

Information use is critical in prioritizing and timing transaction opportunities.

INFORMATION CONTROL IS TIMING POWER

Information control, we'll call it "I-Control," is essential to having and sustaining power. That power is essential at a personal sales level. Data is the capital of today's world, whether it is an international conglomerate or an individual with a laptop. Just ask Bill Gates or Ross Perot.

The Control of America

Much of our economy, even the "old" industries, is driven with information use. Information accumulated, analyzed, and communicated to direct action is *power*. Consider information use on you related to the power possessed in America by:

- **Government/IRS.** The power to mandate law, tax, and to seize assets based on the knowledge provided from tax returns and other asset data sources.

- **Police and Military.** The power to secure society with arms or destroy an enemy based on knowledge of their strengths and weaknesses.

- **Fewer, Bigger Companies.** The power to dominate markets, buy competitors, and set prices based on in-depth knowledge of their consumers.

- **Fewer, Bigger Banks.** The power to create lending decisions based on credit data and less competition.

- **Wall Street.** The power to centralize stock prices based on the accumulation of corporate financial data.

- **Madison Avenue.** The power to influence purchasing habits based on knowledge of the fears and desires of consumers.

- **Credit Bureaus.** The power to positively or negatively report a person's financial status based on the collection of that individual's information from creditors.

Now enter the personal computer. There has never been a personal power tool like it before. What about this information power-source that is available to you?

The Power of the Computer-User

The PC. A *Sales*Mind values the perspective of the previous examples of information power. However, they are even more interested in generating enormous information power with their small, portable laptop or notebook computers that offer almost unlimited software applications. Do you get the most out of your PC or laptop?

If not, invest the time and money and take the training. Give this high priority; you'll find it will be one of your best-ever investments in yourself.

One profitable result is that you will no longer be forced to waste your evenings when you're on the road. Even though most offices are closed, possessing a laptop and knowing how to use it allows you to make this time valuable.

You can send emails to prospects and answer the responses to previous emails that came in during the day. You can also prospect for new sales opportunities by re-searching the Internet using the phone or data connection at your hotel or motel.

The Internet. One of the most awesome societal developments ever is the ability to instantly retrieve infor-mation from anywhere in the world on about any subject from a laptop computer. In fact, you can now do this with handheld devices without plugging into a phone line.

Consider that in 1995, only 11 million people were using the Internet, and 1995 created half of those. By 2001 over 100 million people were Internet users in the U.S and that number will continue to grow by millions each month until it hits saturation. These enormous numbers do not even count the rest of the world's Internet use.

Of course, the dot.com meltdown slowed this trend, which in any case was approaching the saturation level in the world's industrialized nations. Nevertheless, the pressure on salespeople in every field to become constant, capable users of the limitless power of the Internet and computers to maximize income—or merely to remain competitive—will continue to intensify.

These examples demonstrate that the access to and use of knowledge is power. Your question is: What should I be trying to time? What are the highest priorities for which my timing is crucial? Will the successful completion of those priorities be profitable? Do you obtain and use information effectively just like it is being collected and used by organizations to influence and control you?

Critical to those answers for a *Sales*Mind is the possession of enough quantity and quality of information on buyers to make those decisions. You can't time something you don't know about, much less find out how, why, where, and when it operates.

MAKE INFORMATION YOUR KNOWLEDGE

You'll notice that I have shifted from "information" to "knowledge." Organized information control is knowledge. Knowledge used is power.

Information is simply and only neutral data that has the potential for use.

Knowledge though, is the ingestion of information put into practice so that it becomes valuable, solution-based experience. Knowledge matures when it becomes part of the credible judgment a *Sales*Mind uses daily to meet and exceed the expectations of buyers.

Your Acquisition of Specialized Sales Knowledge Makes You Valuable

You might have heard of Curt Schilling, currently a major league baseball pitcher with the Arizona Diamondbacks. He's a perennial all-star and one of the best of all time. He understands the power of specialized knowledge.

A self-described "computer nerd," Schilling spends hours studying a video database of more than 20,000 pitches he has thrown since 1993. On a library of over 100 discs, his laptop charts every pitch he has thrown to almost 500 batters.

He constantly adds to and reviews his data to gain advantages over batters. Is he using information to get results? Just check his wins and salary. Like Curt, a *Sales*Mind is proud to earn top money.

Certainly specialized knowledge, when applied to a viable market for it, is more financially rewarding than merely possessing a wide variety of knowledge.

An eye surgeon makes a great deal more than a smart person who knows lots of things but is not a specialist. A *Sales*Mind is also a specialist and knows there are basically four types of specialized knowledge in relation to the business of selling:

1. **Product, market, and competitive knowledge.** Do you have a daily system to stay on top of your overall business trends?

2. **Sales strategy and tactic knowledge.** Do you study and practice every year the basics, just like an athlete going to training camp?

3. **Buyer knowledge.** Do you search for every possible dimension of what compels your buyers to think, feel, and act the way they do?

4. **Human knowledge.** Most of all, are you thirsty to continuously learn more every day about the make-up and behavior of people?

When you accumulate, coordinate, and sharpen these four types of knowledge, you develop the specialized mindset a *Sales*Mind must possess. Specialized knowledge is conditioned through a total, constant approach to learning.

Specialize Your Knowledge Now, and Give Priority Time to Continuously Adding to It

Specializing knowledge demands constant work to get command of the sharpness of valuable ideas. We have been urged to "do one thing, and do it extremely well." It's also not *what* you know, but what you *do* with what you know that creates impact. No truer words have ever been spoken.

Specialized knowledge is the only kind of information that buyers care about because it's the only kind that (when you use it) has value to them. They probably want it to make some money or feel better. Specialized knowledge yielding value is the primary reason that buyers *call you back and respect you*. Remind yourself of that daily.

*Sales*Minds systematically keep learning and expanding their use of specific, valuable information.

Think about this book's content as an example of that principle.

By reading, watching, listening, and sensing to expand their knowledge, A *Sales*Mind gains detail and expands their perspective. Let's examine a few principles of specializing knowledge:

- **Reading, study, and evaluation.** You will become what your learning program is. What is your learning program? What does it entail? How do you set up your information access?

  Do you read at planned intervals for at least 30 minutes a day? Equally important, are you reading the right things? Also, keep your books and magazines near you. In your next reading session after receiving a selected magazine or trade journal, go through it with a highlighter and scissors and cut out the relevant articles. File them appropriately or at least keep a small box on hand so you can then go through them once per month to use, act on, or permanently file.

  I have done this for many years, and this simple system will offer great benefit to your study program. I read and study. Do you?

- **Information role models.** One of the best moves a *Sales*Mind can make is to find and emulate these models. An information role model is simply an idea or process to willingly emulate. I'm not big on short cuts to anything, but modeling is one. If somebody else (a role model), some institution, or some process has already done masterfully what you are attempting to do, why reinvent the wheel?

Why not study that information model and absorb how it accomplishes I-control? That analysis will help you get the same result factoring in your skills and personality. I have information role models. Do you?

> *"The quality of an idea does not depend on its altitude in the organization. An idea can come from any source. So we will search the globe for ideas."*
> —— **Jack Welch,**
> Former General Electric CEO
> and author of *The GE Way*.

- **Personal role models.** Go back to your values. Your role models should have the value system that matches yours. Make a role model list and let it build as others come to mind. Define in writing exactly what attributes you aspire to and admire in your role models. Are they character traits? Are they skills?

Maybe your role models are religious leaders, parents, your spouse, presidents, authors, soldiers, coaches, scout masters, former managers, the top *Sales*Mind in your company, or other business mentors. Make your own private list of people.

I'll list some of mine: Jesus Christ, my wife, my parents, Ronald and Nancy Reagan, Mother Teresa, Larry Bird, Michael Jordan, Wilt Chamberlain, Douglas McArthur, Lou Holtz, Rush Limbaugh, George Washington, Abraham Lincoln, Billy Graham, Galileo, Edison, Einstein, and many more.

As a kid, didn't you imagine growing up and being like someone? This is the adult version. Cut out pictures and read bios. Be focused and watch a person in an experience or circumstance for the purpose of modeling their behavior. I have a vast assortment of people, past and present, who I respect and model. Do you?

- **Seminars.** They blend information with motivation. You can listen, watch, write notes, interact, and get the high points of a professional's perspective to the topics you need to grow. You are also in a company of others, which always heightens and gives credibility to learning. Not only do I give seminars every week, I go to every one I can. Do you?

- **Multi-media learning.** Recall Curt Schilling? Use all the current technology like CDs, videos, DVDs, web-based programs, Internet learning universities, and hand-held wireless devices like he does to enhance results. Today's interactive information has been designed to be very effective and learning-efficient. In this flexible and personal learning world:

  - **You can learn at home on your own time.**

  - **You can reinforce your live seminar training and reading.**

  - **You can learn in conjunction with remote coaching or study partners.**

- **Your learning can tie in with your manager's assistance and field coaching.**

- **You can use learning programs that until recently were unavailable, inaccessible, or prohibitively expensive.**

"I believe that if you read enough about something, you're going to unravel its mystery, and will ultimately understand the fundamentals in a deeper way than simple observation would provide. Then, if you have an inquiring mind, you can apply yourself to that subject and have success in ways not experienced even by those who have spent much more time on it."

—— **Rudolph Giuliani,**
Former New York mayor
in his book, *Leadership*

I learn everywhere, grow, and make money with the influence of personal media. Do you?

Sales*Minds *use specialized knowledge to enhance their timing.

USE INFORMATION CONTROL TOOLS

I-Tools comprise any tangible equipment, systems, and structures at your disposal. They help you serve buyers, make money, save time, increase efficiency, and make your life easier. Our world has been affected so dramatically by the rapid succession of I-Tools. It's staggering how much business and information you can manage from one hand-held device.

The Tools Are Everywhere

No one has an excuse today for a lack of access to affordable tools and systems to help you control your information. There are so many tools:

- **Basic office stationary tools.** Files, calendars, scheduling boards, lists, etc.

- **Portable paper tools.** Planners, notebooks, reports, Post-Its ®, etc.

- **Electronic tools.** Personal and laptop computers, hand-held computers, servers with databases, cell phones, etc.

The list is endless, and from this writing, many new tools will be added. The bottom line is that on the market today is every possible tool a *Sales*Mind needs to control information.

> *"**Order.** Let all your things have their places. Let each part of your business have its time."*
> —— **Benjamin Franklin**
> Number 3 of his 13 Virtues.

Control Your Information Life

I-Tools are the structures that enable you to have:

- A place for your responsibilities.
- A place for your priorities.
- A place for your detail.
- A place for your goals and deadlines.
- A place for your buyer profiles.
- A place for your timing cycles to operate.

*In addition to rendering service, Sales**Minds** use the timing advantages of I-Tools to save time and money, and make their own lives easier.*

THE STAGES OF I-CONTROL

Every bit of data, whether you are aware that it exists or not, has a relationship to you. The price of tea in China or the size of the moose herd in Canada may be irrelevant, so that relationship is *irrelevancy*. But for the information that is relevant to your sales business, that information has three successive stages or states of existence:

First, Raw Information

Do you have files or piles (of files)? I thought so. You know, that pile of stuff on the corner of everybody's desk that just keeps growing until, about once a year, the pile tumbles onto the floor some night and the night janitor throws it into the trash. In many average sales departments, numerous sparkling sales opportunities meet such a premature end. How many unmade sales are lying on your desk?

Information is in a raw, or undeveloped state when you either don't possess it, or have it but can't find it when needed. Even if you possess some valuable business information and can retrieve it when needed, it's useless if you do nothing with it. Ask these questions about the raw data in your world:

- **Existent but distant?** You are aware that highly useful information exists in a database or some other source not on-hand or available to you. For example, the industry association list you need but haven't accessed. Actually, in many cases a few minutes thought will reveal an honorable way to obtain the desired data.

- **Inaccessible?** You can't get to all desired data. For example, you probably can't access data on the exact purchases and transactions of all buyers in your category.

- **Retrievable?** You must identify the exact (purchase or download) process for acquiring the data you want to access.

- **Sorted?** You must categorize and code the data you retrieve for outgoing use (contact).

Second, Operational Information

You have to make information *move*. Get it off your desk, off of cards and Post-Its, and into a cyclical electronic format with an outgoing flow. Like all modeling, is there an entity or person who has a process that already exists to deal with how you need your data to operate? Raw information becomes operational when it is actively being used to answer these types of questions:

- **Plans.** What goals, market niches, ideas, objectives, and priorities should I pursue?

- **Assumptions.** Why am I or we doing the things we do to get buyers?

- **Decisions.** How is my upside/downside thinking enriched to take action?

- **Actions.** What is the next step to take now in the sales process with a buyer?

- **Evaluations.** What happened on that sales call or in that account this year?

- **Adjustments.** What do I have to do to beat forecast and make more money?

Third, Profitable Information (Considering "The Use Test")

When information is operational, it will provide a gratifying return on your investment of time and money to acquire it. This happens when it creates buyer response or enables service. If information is truly under control, it has to answer these five questions and pass what I call, "The Use Test:"

1. Do you have it and can access it quickly for use?

2. Do you place it in a format you can understand and act on?

3. Do you convert it into an item of influence like an email, letter, or phone call to buyers?

4. Do you execute—get the converted information out to a buyer?

5. Do you have a trigger system to accomplish follow-up with it?

Operational information used by a SalesMind is a gold mine in timing opportunities, but is worthless when unused.

Control is the *flow* of timing. It is the bloodstream of information that nourishes your business and reveals sales and relationship opportunities. But your information stream has to have a far enough reach and impact or your sales machine will be too small. So next up you'll find a valuable insurance policy that will guarantee one of two conditions for you—success or failure. It's your choice.

11

COVERAGE

GO WIDE

McDonald's won't miss your business if you go on a personal boycott and refuse to buy their products. They've sold billions of burgers, and will sell billions more. But if you consider the effect of high fat foods on your life expectancy, you might eat elsewhere.

- Your body has miles upon miles of arteries, veins, and capillaries that bring nourishing blood to every cell of your body. It's an incredible feat because the average adult human body consists of ten trillion cells. Laid end to end, they would circle the globe almost 50 times.

- A single radio signal can feed hundreds of thousands of listeners wherever there is a radio tuned to that frequency.

- The Internet puts instant information in the hands of billions of people.

- Wal-Mart, Home Depot, or General Motors can put a supplier on the map or out of business.

- The oil companies dictate what price I pay for gasoline because where else am I going to buy it?

What is common here? The power and impact of *coverage*.

COVERAGE IS THE SCOPE OF TIMING

Coverage is defined as " to occupy the area of or to extend over." As a *Sales*Mind, you are a sales soldier, and you *occupy* your territory. In the sales world, coverage of a market creates influence on a certain quantity of potential buyers. It is your realm of influence. But, if a potential buyer in your territory is unaware of you, your company, or your product, they don't count in that realm. Remember quantity (wide) leverage from chapter 8? Coverage of your area or market creates that quantity leverage.

Withdraw Your Cash: Leverage Enough Buyers

Dollars must first be loaded into a cash machine before they can be taken out. Your cash machine is your sales business. It is loaded with dollars (income) in the form of buyers, geography, and information from which you have to establish profitable priorities. A *Sales*Mind must also have wide enough territory and account coverage to collect a base of information to establish those priorities. When you intensely pursue your priorities with sales effort and skill, you start withdrawing cash.

A *Sales*Mind knows that achieving that condition requires time spent generating raw numbers of potential buyers. When the necessary width exists, *Sales*Minds have a critical mass of potential buyers from which they can identify and pursue the accounts with the potential to provide the highest yield. If that width does not exist, how reliable is your judgment of having discovered the best accounts with the most revenue and profit potential? You have to call on *enough* potential buyers to know who the *best* are.

Coverage is not just prospecting. It is a *total business strategy for success*. Coverage is grounded in the daily awareness of how many sales dollars are in your sales pipeline, which is your cash machine. You must have the constant commitment to expand and control your sales terrain.

Your Cut of the Money

Up to a point, *Sales*Minds want all the marketing they can get to support their sales efforts. There is nothing as lonely as selling without marketing support. Selling then becomes very hard work. It's like ground troops trying to fight without air cover and support. I said, "up to a point." That point is where your company spends so much money on marketing that there is less commission for you when sales are closed. This aspect of earning personal income from selling operates on these two coverage principles:

Principle One: *The less responsibility you have for getting new business, the less money you will make.* You may not get many or any leads from marketing. You're not the first *Sales*Mind to plead that case. Everyone wants more leads to sell. It's easier. You don't have to apply the prospecting effort. You won't have an uncertain return on the investment of your courage, time, and resources. You're not faced with handling the resistance of new buyers. Let the company spend money to put leads on your desk. You'll just close them.

Sounds great, right? However, this pretty picture comes with a problem: because you're less valuable, you won't make as much commission as a percentage of each transaction. In other words, when the marketing cost eats up a higher percentage of the selling price, less money is left to pay you a commission. In these situations, leverage is on the side of your company.

Principle Two: *The more responsibility you have for getting new business, the more money you will make.* Why? Because you're being paid for those marketing and prospecting efforts instead of the same money going to advertising agencies, trade shows, direct mail expenses, and the like for marketing costs. Your coverage efforts are those costs.

I'll illustrate this principle through my first sales experience right out of college: Selling copiers door to door. I was assigned a territory with very few existing accounts. The company did very little marketing to generate leads for me. Their job proposition to me was, "If you pay your own expenses, make twenty cold calls a day, and cover your territory, we'll train you in the selling skills it takes to develop and close sales." And they did.

That experience was the best thing they could have ever done for me to teach me how to sell. I had to find my own buyers, so I did. My commissions were also higher because my sales efforts were most of their marketing costs. It was a fair trade. This conditioning and experience was also invaluable when I left and started my own training business. The first thing I did was go back to my old copier customers and train their salespeople.

These two principles reveal how you and your company leverage each other. The decisive question is, "Who has the positional advantage of bringing in most or all of the leads?"

However, I want to stress that in this day and time of low buyer attention and high competition, *Sales*Minds *want all the effective marketing they can get.* But they never just leave the vital functions of marketing, prospecting, and networking up to the company or distributors *alone.* If you relinquish all those efforts, you lose leverage and become a lower-paid order-taker.

*SalesMinds **combine marketing, distributors, and personal effort to have coverage with enough buyers to generate wide leverage.***

LEVERAGE THE BEST BUYERS FOR PRICE

While coverage determines your total buyer leverage, there is another key relationship it ultimately establishes. I call it securing the "best buyer." The best buyer is the buyer you have the best relationship with and who pays the highest price for your product or service.

But first you have to find the best buyer, and their price results from a negotiation with you. Your stance in that negotiation was based on a leverage position of value and high service. Remember, *your highest contribution of service for a buyer is your strongest component of leverage.*

It's very important to review and build on the steps to get to a leveraged price position with your best buyers:

- **You leverage each buyer.** First, you remember that quality leverage occurs one relationship at a time. Remember to deepen relationship leverage with each priority buyer.

- **You leverage total buyers.** Second, quantity leverage is the total amount of buyers under your influence at any one time. The goal is to increase your business leverage by having enough buyers to influence within your available time.

- **You secure your best buyers.** Third, now that you have enough potential buyers, focus on identifying the best of those buyers. Separate the wheat from the chaff. Think of it this way. How would you know that you have the best possible buyers until you have seen enough of them to compare and make that determination? Remember that your priorities and information control are assisting you in these choices.

- **You leverage price with all best buyers.** Fourth, when you are wide enough to have determined the best possible buyers, you have the leverage to negotiate the best price and terms with each of them. That leverage exists because you are not too reliant on the revenue from any one buyer. Your stance is one of strength because of your coverage.

Please—

In so many years of sales and training, I have both made and seen the mistake of stopping at a limited level of potential buyers and never going on to find the other choice accounts (best buyers) that explode commissions. Don't fall into that trap. Set a simple coverage goal. For example, if it takes seeing two new buyers a week for ten weeks to see twenty new potential buyers, do it. Persistent effort—such as all budding *Sales*Minds eagerly embark upon and stick with—guarantees wide leverage. It's well worth the effort because it leads straight to maximum earnings.

***SalesMinds** go wide to discover enough total buyers to give them price leverage with the best buyers.*

BELIEVE IN COVERAGE RESULTS

You must believe that the income you seek will happen if you work in an urgent and skilled fashion. Go back to Action (Chapter 3) where we discussed the effect of cumulative action. This aspect of action is based on this truism: A mass of, for example, twenty coverage actions by you—even with low beginning information—will result in some percentage of transactions. You just don't know *which* of the twenty will become the result. The same premise applies here:

It's vital to execute your day believing you will get powerful sales results **if enough buyers are:**

- Aware of your program—
- Qualified for your program—
- Persuaded by your program—then…
- **Transactions will occur.**

*Sales***Minds also believe that even higher leverage occurs when they—**

- Stay sharp by practicing new-buyer contact skills.
- Manage the risk that any current buyers will leave them, buy from someone else, and therefore erode their ability to meet sales goals.

- Introduce a new product or develop a new relationship.
- Introduce a new person in his or her own company to the buyer relationship.
- Create add-on sales or expand an existing relationship.
- Acquire referrals from their coverage efforts.

In reverse—and I don't want to be negative—but you also better believe you will have low leverage because of lack of all of the above.

An essential SalesMind *belief: influencing many buyers has multiple benefits.*

*SALES*MINDS MAKE COLD CALLS

They Visit People

Many salespeople today either do not or can't make a cold call. Some only call on the comfortable buyers they know; others expect marketing to provide leads that take the cold out of the call. One of my sales mentors told me, "Forget about considering this a cold call; just think of it as visiting people." That little nugget of advice totally changed the way I viewed new calls. I challenge you today to focus on, practice, and execute the following contact process to get in front of a new buyer:

1. **The objective:** Your goal is to set an appointment with a key decision-maker for a twenty-minute appointment in your market area, period. Commit to it.

2. **The first phone calls:** Expect to make four to five phone calls within a thirty-day period to succeed. Your phone call is like a commercial. It takes consistent repetition to have effect. In considering this, factor in reality: the buyer you're trying to reach may not even be in the office, or may otherwise be unavailable, when you call.

3. **The screen:** A secretary answers. For convenience, we're going to assume the secretary is a woman although today more and more secretaries are men. "Good morning," you politely say, "I am Doug Trenary with DTFast-Track, Inc. Is Mr. Johnson available to speak for just a moment?" You are of course screened and told he is in a meeting. With the screener/secretary, you have these goals:

   • Pleasantly agree to go into the voice mail with no frustration, and then—

   • Ask her name and repeat it back to her. Thank her for her time and attention.

   • Ask her if there is an exact or best time she knows he will be in and perhaps can talk.

   • Ask her if she can set a short appointment with you for him. Your kindness with her is vital because remember you are going to be calling (her) back very shortly. Tell her kindly to expect this call back.

4. **The voice mail:** You get Mr. Johnson's greeting. At the beep you again announce yourself and professionally state that you would like to see him for about twenty minutes to introduce yourself and the value of your program. State any credibility points of yours quickly, leave your number clearly to invite his call, but assure him you will call back in a few day if you do not hear from him.

Key: Your voice mail is an "audio commercial" that presents you, your attitude, and your voice. Make sure it presents your qualities and values in their best possible light. With that view in mind, speak clearly and with enthusiasm. Never let any hint of frustration creep into your audio commercial about being subjected to the voice mail screen. Keep in mind that all Mr. Johnson has to go on as he decides whether or not to see you is what you say and— even more importantly—how you say it.

Also keep this in mind: Voice mail screens *discourage* average salespeople, most of whom never call back, which is why busy decision makers love them. Voice mail is a reality that *Sales*Minds know how to work for maximum benefit, and they know this requires patience. After leaving your audio commercial on Mr. Johnson's voice mail, go to your software tickler and key in your phone-back date, which should be within a few days.

5. **The decision-maker:** You keep calling politely and persistently. Finally on your fifth call, you get Mr. Johnson: "Thanks for your calls, Doug....I have just been real busy, and it would be hard to get together right now—"

6. **The objection response:** "Mr. Johnson, I understand, and all of my clients with busy schedules began in one small step with me....just about twenty minutes to introduce the ideas and value behind our product _____. I'd be happy to come first thing in the morning over a cup of coffee or last thing in the day. May I come in for just a few minutes this week for that introduction?" Keep your words going without hesitation or interruption. You get agreement, and set the appointment. You are always sitting in that office ten minutes early.

7. **The appointment:** When you meet Mr. Johnson, your goal is connection. Go back to Connection (chapter 5) and review those skills, particularly the discussion of input (questions and listening).

The above may not precisely represent the ideal cold-call scenario for your product or service. In other words, you may need to adapt it to fit your style and offering. I challenge you to try this approach ten times and tell me it *doesn't* work. Even if you don't use my flow, just the practice will enable you to have the courage and skill to get in front of people.

Determine Follow-Up Triggers

Another constant dimension of coverage is follow-up or reconnection. You have now made contact, and perhaps a first appointment or two. One of your key timing goals is to discover and record the information that tells you where the enzymes of the transaction are. I call these "follow-up triggers."

Follow-up triggers enhance your timing when calling back. Where priority accounts or activities are established, the triggers allow you to be there early enough or at the right time to get the business. There are some questions that can help you establish these triggers:

- When are key decision-maker meetings?

- Is there a seasonality factor that predicts early buying?

- Is there a previous buying history that tells me clearly about purchasing timing, quantity, and profitability?

- Is there budget information to tell me when there is allocation and release of dollars?

- Will decisions regarding the purchase be made in a committee meeting? If so, when will it be held?

- Is there a trial or testing period for my products that I can leverage for a review and potential decision in my favor?

- Have I been referred to talk to someone else in the buyer's organization?

These are just a few examples of the kind of questions that will help you establish the follow-up triggers. The bits of data they uncover will guide you toward better timing of your follow-up efforts. Timing is vital. Get there too soon and they won't reach a decision; get their too late and it's already made and, chances are, your competitor has walked away with the business. Make sure you start identifying a general list of your own triggers, and then apply that list to get answers for each buyer.

*Sales*Minds *make cold calls and then collect information to help them zero in on the most profitable time to follow-up.*

BE SMART WITH YOUR COVERAGE

Smart coverage means *consistently using your resources wisely.* Besides bringing your whole array of selling skills to bear, using your resources wisely involves applying a mix of methods to contact buyers. It also calls for you to generate greater marketing impact with a desktop or laptop computer, and to use such other modern technology to do more in less time.

Do You Allocate Your Resources Wisely?

*Sales*Minds use all their resources wisely and efficiently. These may be resources of the company plus their own personal resources. Ask these questions of yourself about the resources and assets you can invest in your coverage and persuasion efforts:

- **Information.** How many information management resources are available to me in computer equipment, software applications, and processes to sort out information?

- **Experience.** How much valuable experience do I bring to the buyer?

- **Management.** How much valuable experience does my boss or others in the company bring to the buyer?

- **Money.** How much money are we investing in marketing and awareness?

- **Time.** How much time (including travel time) do I need and have to cover my market area?

- **Energy.** Do I have the daily energy needed to cover my area?

This kind of assessment gives a *Sales*Mind a strong perspective on how they will allocate their corporate and personal resources in pursuit of their coverage goals.

Mix It Up

When you have made decisions about your coverage resources, you must employ a "contact mix." That mix is exactly how you execute the individual tactical contacts to cover accounts and geography.

To get buyer attention, a *Sales*Mind has to contact a buyer in a multitude of ways to unlock that attention and not be repetitive with any one type of contact. For example, if your *only* method of new buyer contact is the phone, then that buyer gets immune to your repeated phone calls. Your contacts must come from different angles and from multiple devices:

- **Vary your efforts.** Your in–person visits, phone calls, personal letters, emails, and personal notes should all be mixed together in your coverage efforts. In other words, you might first call and have conversations or leave some voice mails. Then mix that up with your email dialogue, then an occasional letter or fax. Then mix that up with a periodic company or personal mail piece. This contact mix is very effective because it holds and even builds buyer attention. You are not overusing any one medium and will find the right mental angle in the buyer by involving their different senses.

- **Be a desk-top marketer.** Put your PC to work by establishing a personal web page. You might also generate powerful visuals or slides, or include short, persuasive email attachments. However, attach-ments on emails are a common vehicle for transmitting viruses, so many people will not open them. You can get around this smoothly by simply copying the attachment and pasting it into the body of the email. Generating greater coverage output with a computer is a must today for a *Sales*Mind.

- **Have a website.** In all my years of business, our website **www.dougtrenary.com** has by far been the greatest tool to grow our business. Go log on and take a look! It generates endless exposure and links us to partners and buyers. It also allows me to provide and update my content for those who log on. The possibilities a website creates are unlimited.

*From their PC or in the field, Sales**Minds** **allocate their resources wisely and mix up their types of contact for creative impact on the buyer.***

Coverage is the *scope* of timing. It is the action variable that determines the total amount of business landscape for your influence and timing. Your landscape though, will constantly change. But the issue is not whether or not your personal and sales worlds change. Rather, it's whether you will continue to refine your thoughts and efforts to win like the following guys did whose products you probably now use every day.

12

ADJUSTMENT

MCCLELLAN ON THE FIFTY

B ill Gates and Paul Allen of Microsoft initiated groundbreaking societal adjustments beginning in 1976. Those adjustments helped computer-users make countless further adjustments that have changed the world. The needs occurring in both computer/software buyers and sellers had opened a market whose size dwarfed anything previously seen.

These changes were moving at the speed of light compared to the pace of change in traditional industries.

They knew that to tap into the massive opportunity of expanding computer-users, and to maintain and expand their company's position, they had to supply the user with a simplified method of operating a computer to replace the complicated DOS key commands.

The best idea available at the time was Apple's point-and-click concept, so they adjusted quickly to maintain their competitiveness and borrowed or appropriated the concept from Apple. Neither word expresses the process accurately since Apple still had full use of the concept they had originated. This was in the tradition of Henry Ford, who often incorporated innovations made by other companies into his automobiles, farm equipment, and aircraft.

Such things often happen in business worldwide, but that's another story. However, it's well worth noting how this plays out in the marketplace. In and of itself, which company originates a new development doesn't count for much; far more important is who maximizes the opportunities available with a given product.

Apple, by the way, had borrowed the concept from Xerox, who thought it was useless at the time. (I'd like to know where the executives responsible for that decision are working now.)

So when Gates and Allen introduced the adjustment of Windows point-and-click operation to the vastly larger customer base for IBM-type computers, they knew millions of current users would soon convert to the easier-to-operate new operating system. Moreover, millions of first-time buyers would discover that they could operate personal computers, and the explosive world-changing reality of Microsoft's second explosive growth period was born.

They hoped they would be right, and they were. Needless to say, they and countless others pocketed some dollars as a result of the market's response to their adjustment. The Microsoft story was all about causing an adjustment to a dynamic already in play (computer use) and capitalizing on change at the right time (timing) in a way that influenced buyers to buy.

ADJUSTMENT IS THE CHANGE OF TIMING

Adjustment is defined as "to change, correct, adapt, conform, or regulate as to match, fit or bring into proper relationship." If you try something repeatedly without getting the desired result, what should your response be? Continue doing the same thing that doesn't work? Change something?

If you continue doing something without getting the results you want, the ultimate foolishness is to *keep* doing that same thing in hopes of getting a different, more favorable, result.

That's folly of vast proportions. The world saw this recently when the UN, after trying for eleven years to persuade Saddam Hussein to reform with one fierce but impotent resolution after another, demanded that the brutal dictator be given a few more months. Declining to continue with fruitless tactics, the United States and the United Kingdom adjusted and formed a coalition to solve the threat to world peace with action that yielded the desired result in three weeks.

"The strength of a plan is the ability to adjust to circumstances as you stay focused on an objective."
——**General Vincent Brooks**
CentCom Briefing on "Operation Iraqi Freedom"

Adjustment. Changing is never easy. But *Sales*-Minds in pursuit of ever-higher results realizes they may need to change something in their plan or efforts before they run out of time or get brushed aside by people who are quick to embrace change. A *Sales*Mind understands:

- Making adjustments is time related; the period of opportunity in which to get results is limited. Unfortunately, that time is usually shorter than one anticipates, and it's often only known after the window of opportunity is slammed shut by competitors who are faster on their feet.

- The purpose of making adjustments or changes is to accomplish more effective timing of our actions.

- Timing is taking an effective action at the best possible moment to get the maximum desired result.

A *Sales*Mind must constantly make adjustments in their plan because of the combination of mistakes, unknowns, and the effect of constant external changes. In doing so, their timing process is constantly modified in pursuit of their opportunities.

"You're going to make a lot of mistakes, and you have to be open to changing your course."
—— **Bill Gates**

Whether *Sales*Minds make a personal adjustment or capitalize on a buyer change, the element of **time** is involved in:

- **Awareness.** The need to change is constant and *timeless*. Gates and Allen knew that the computer market was churning with constant change. A *Sales*Mind knows that their buyers in general are constantly looking for ways to make money, reduce costs, look good, and have more emotional satisfaction.

- **Identification.** Recognizing buyer opportunities demands *timeliness*. Gates and Allen evaluated and identified that the key to expanding the computer usage market was to make the computer program easy to access and use for the buyer. A *Sales*Mind looks for specific ways to help a buyer by knowing that buyer's business and personal profile.

- **Realization.** It can only happen when your ego permits you to get a clear-eyed view of the fact that it's *time* to make a change of some degree. A *Sales*Mind knows when to admit that the old or current approach is no longer the most effective approach to get maximum results. Gates and Allen knew that without organizing the widest possible marketing partnerships, they could not market the Windows concept fast enough to quickly establish dominance. *Sales*Minds know how easy it is to get stuck in a rut, lose their freshness and enthusiasm, and see their former competitive edge with their buyers evaporate like a morning mist—sometimes as quickly.

- **Action.** The release of action to the right buyers with a modified idea or approach, which is *timing*. Gates and Allen approached and struck a deal with IBM just as IBM was growing the market for personal computers and needed an easier operating system. A *Sales*Mind constantly makes changes, some very subtle and some major, to get maximum results.

- **Reality.** You must get results from an adjustment within a *timetable*, a deadline. Gates and Allen didn't have the luxury of waiting around to affect these changes. They jumped on it and got it done. Your sales bonus, quota, and month-end deadlines won't wait for you either. When change is imminent, take action now, today, this minute.

Several history-changing instances of enormous—but only briefly open—opportunities took place during the American Civil War. The most egregious occurred when the South invaded Maryland in 1862. A copy of Lee's orders to the widely dispersed elements of the Confederate Army fell into the hands of McClellan, commanding general of the Northern Army. Had McClellan acted quickly, he could have destroyed Lee's Army of Northern Virginia. But McClellan did nothing until the next day, by which time Lee, who had been promptly informed of the situation, had taken action to assemble his scattered army. McClellan's inaction meant the war would continue for another 31 bloody months.

President Abraham Lincoln soon adjusted by firing McClellan and continuing his search for a fighting general who would produce victories. Had McClellan acted quickly that day in 1862, his face would be on our $50 bill instead of U.S. Grant's.

In business, it is not who knows something or even when they know it. Rather, it is who does something with what they know at the right time who reaps the reward.

INTELLIGENT PERSISTENCE

I spend a lot of time on airplanes. Have you ever thought about the countless adjustments that have been made from the original Wright brother's biplane to the F-16? Many intelligent engineers and pilots have persisted in their designs and testing to accomplish these remarkable results.

As a *Sales*Mind, there are also multitudes of reasons to adjust your thoughts, emotions, and actions. The three together produce results, and a *Sales*Mind must be a constant evaluator and adjuster of *what gets results*. Every *Sales*Mind has had activities that yielded limited results as well as activities that are consistent winners.

I call this awareness and adjusting "intelligent persistence." It is the knowledge of what to add or subtract in order to reach a goal. It's like getting off the main railroad track onto a sidetrack and then getting back on the main track to your destination again. And because some strategies work better than others, you have to make constant adjustments to your plans, ideas, and relationships.

Consider a few more examples of lack of adjustment leading to failure:

- The makers of hats in the 1950s didn't see the trend toward going hatless in America soon enough to adjust by starting to manufacture other kinds of apparel. By the 1960s the hat makers had vanished. Oddly enough, hats are back in style.

- Parliament and King George III didn't realize the counter-productivity of their taxation, religious persecution, censorship, and arrogance toward the thirteen English colonies in North America. The result: the Colonies revolted and became the United States by winning our War for Independence.

- Few retailers were able to adjust to the dominance of Wal-Mart, and American retailing changed forever.

Successful Adjustments Are Everywhere

Examine almost any aspect of your surroundings, and you'll see that changes and adjustments are constantly occurring in every area of our lives.

- The seasons are in a constant change, the days growing longer every day until they reach their maximum length and then begin to grow shorter in an endlessly repeated cycle.

- Societies and governments adjust to changing social demands.

- Economies and markets are always in a state of flux as they adjust to meet the constantly changing levels and complex interactions of worldwide supply of— and demand for—commodities, products, and services of every kind.

- Families adjust as parents age and children grow.

- When behind on the scoreboard, successful sports teams adjust at halftime. At other times they adjust personnel due to the financial demands of player contracts.

> *"But one thing I do: Forgetting what is behind and straining toward what is ahead."*
> —— **Philippians 3:13**

Why Should You Adjust?

A *Sales*Mind uses this worldly awareness to validate their focus on business adjustments. Knowing that adjustments must be constant and of varying degrees, you may need adjustments for any of these reasons:

- To simplify your sales presentation, better fitting a buyer's real need.
- To react to adjustments in your buyer, competition, market, economy, or innovation that require that you respond with personal change.

- To adjust your actions because your plans and performances are not achieving the results you want.
- To find out more about a buyer's personal life in order to enhance connection.
- To correct with urgent, caring service a problem your company is responsible for.
- To soften your communication style to create more comfort with a tentative buyer.
- To rethink your market position in a changing economy.
- To ask thoughtful questions and listen carefully to the answers to better navigate the buying process.
- To react to a buyer's verbal response.
- To perform within priorities and limited time because you can't adjust to everything.
- To overcome the limits of your own ego.
- To overcome current behaviors that are engrained and hard to change.
- To handle short-term setbacks.
- To counter behavior and attitudes which are less than your best.

Producing top sales results is a demanding undertaking that is well worth the effort required. One of those key demands is for a *Sales*Mind to understand the daily, multi-layered reasoning for making changes.

*A Sales**Mind** observes successful adjustments everywhere as the rationale to apply intelligent persistence.*

ADJUST TO HELP BUYERS

Helping buyers is our purpose. But knowing how, why, and when to help them is another matter. A *Sales*Mind has to acquire the stimuli and information it takes to help in the best possible way.

Triggers for Change

A "trigger" is any system to receive feedback for the purpose of putting action into motion. You should ask three questions to develop information triggers that will present change for the buyer's good:

1. Do you examine the original objectives documented by you and your company to serve the buyer's needs? If they are not being met, this triggers a *Sales*Mind to take action that will move customer service adjustments back to plan.

2. Do you examine assessments from the viewpoint of control and coverage? A *Sales*Mind may uncover information about a buyer problem or about a new prospect. That information triggers them into action to solve a problem or pursue an opportunity.

3. Do you know exactly why positive adjustments affecting the buyer should be initiated? A *Sales*Mind has an information system to illuminate three timing scenarios to trigger changes that help buyers. One type is *proactive*, the other two are *reactive*:

Anticipation

This calls for proactive analysis *before buyers know we can help them*. It answers this question: How can we help our buyers with the feedback we have before they are caught short by changes that will impact them significantly?

On the upside. We help them by anticipating their needs and making adjustments as a seller. Our analysis of a problem or opportunity in the market allows us to recommend new ideas and to have time for both parties to react to change.

Our goal is to anticipate a turn of events and help engineer a response change proactively, thus the term "anticipation."

On the downside. If we fail to anticipate the impact of an important change (for example, a technological development in our area of expertise) in some cases our customers may blame us for the pain the change causes them. In some situations, failures of this kind can decimate your customer base.

Pharmaceutical companies provide a good example. For years, their research was showing cholesterol levels of Americans on the rise, which is a major factor in heart disease. Through investment and research, the drug companies created and released cholesterol-reducing drugs that are very effective. They anticipated the scale of this problem and made adjustments to help both doctors and patients.

Overall, analysis for proactive adjustment is a scenario in which *Sales*Minds know their buyers, their buyers' customers, and their overall business and industry. They also know the context of their buyers' business in the economy at large.

Needless to say, *Sales*Minds have the best buyer relationships because they are more in touch than run-of-the-mill salespeople. They are also the most valuable to their buyers, and as a consequence, make the most money. Any time change can be anticipated and responded to in a timely fashion by the seller, value is created for the buyer.

Innovation

This refers to reactive analysis *before buyers have helped themselves.*

How can we help our buyers with feedback we have and that they could have (but may not have digested yet) regarding the variables of change? By analysis of an outcome after it happens, you can still make an adjustment before the buyer calls you to make changes.

This scenario is still effective because *Sales*Minds have structures in place to get market feedback and make swift adjustments. I term this "innovation" because this scenario allows for new improvements to be offered to the buyer before they really feel the pain of a problem.

For example, my Internet Service Provider recently launched a free "anti-spam" program, placed it on their server, and then informed me of the new service. I was just to the point where I was getting annoyed by the junk email and would soon have explored how to filter it out.

Irritation was beginning to set in, but my provider was ahead of me. I have been delighted with the value of their innovation. Any time positive change is first initiated by the seller (even when the buyers know their own problems), this action creates value for the buyer.

Expectation

Expectation refers to reaction *after we should (unknowingly) have already helped them.*

How can we help our buyers when we get feedback from them that we need to make changes to help them? In this scenario, you learn from the buyers of new or sudden changes in the conditions that face your buyers. You then make a change.

This is a level of response a buyer would expect, thus the term, "expectation." The difference here is that there was an ineffective system of analysis in place to look for problems or issues of necessary change affecting your buyer. The feedback originated from a system that the *buyer*, not you the seller, put in place.

For example, you are unaware of the fact that one of your 200 stores has had late deliveries on a certain product. The buyer lets you know, and you move immediately to solve the shipping problem. That's their minimum expectation. The downside is they have already been adversely affected to some degree. Remember, another competitive seller may have a better, more proactive feedback system than you to offer your buyers, particularly if they have felt high pain. You could be replaced.

Sales*Minds *use information analysis for timing adjustments that help their buyers.

JUST EVALUATE

Thomas Edison revolutionized the world by continuing to adjust his experiments until the electric light bulb became a reality of phenomenal impact. He knew he was moving in the right direction with his experiments because he used two interlocking types of evaluation to yield feedback.

The first was *quantitative,* which means to measure in numbers or units. Can you imagine how many times he changed ever so slightly the exact measurement of a chemical or degree of a condition within the glass bulb?

The second was *qualitative,* which means his observation, comparisons, and intuition regarding the result of each experiment. After thousands of experiments the *light came on* because of these two types of evaluation.

> *"The intuitive mind is a sacred gift,*
> *and the rational mind is a faithful servant.*
> *We have created a society that honors the servant*
> *and has forgotten the gift."*
> —— **Albert Einstein**

You Have to Ask Questions

When you have created a first result, take that information, evaluate it, and then make an action adjustment to get a second result. Be aware that at some point in the future, that second result will be evaluated and adjusted again. Then do this process again and again. Remind yourself of Edison and all of the evaluations and adjustments he used to create the world's first electric light bulb.

*Sales*Minds can learn from the scientist, the great athlete, or the star performer. *Sales*Minds can learn from the coaches who make adjustments in the second half and win the game, from the generals who adjust their tactics from battle to battle and win their wars, or from CEOs who adjust their companies' R & D and dominate an emerging technology.

*Sales*Minds set up questions that yield key feedback when answered. Here is a sample of questions for the sales business:

Quantitative Evaluation Questions

1. As an average, how many buyer presentations does it take for you make one sale?
2. How many new sales calls need to be added weekly to meet and exceed a sales forecast?
3. Out of every 10 phone calls, how many actually reach the targeted contact?

Qualitative Evaluation Questions

1. Is my sales approach too aggressive or too passive?
2. Is my attitude fundamentally positive or negative?
3. Is my strategy in line with others who are highly successful?

A *Sales*Mind develops the balance of measuring outcomes by both numbers and intuition.

Sales*Minds *establish both numerical and intuitive evaluation to instigate adjustments for better timing. That is, they use both number crunching and gut feelings to improve their timing.

ADJUST YOUR DEGREES OF ACTION

Adjustments by you or your company need to be planned when possible. More importantly, they must occur by action. But needed adjustments have degrees or levels of the severity of action.

Should You Polish It or Have Surgery?

Sometimes you do something well and the only adjustment is to *maintain* that performance and keep it polished. On the opposite scale, you may have been trying to force a plan to work for years, with nothing but losses. This is the total adjustment of *absolute, complete change.* It's major surgery.

In the processing of information, the *Sales*Mind understands evaluation's role. Evaluation of what you have done allows you to review information, experiences, logic, emotions, goals, and performances for potential adjustment.

It's a Matter of Degree

When an evaluation has been completed, employ any of these five degrees of adjustment:

1. **Keep succeeding** (least adjustment) because the goal reached was finely performed. Simply replicate and expand your performance. Refine by polishing performance. Don't get comfortable.

2. **Make adjustments** of fuel to the equation to increase the rate of results. Add more money, time, and energy resources to the same process. You may just need to move faster.

3. **Moderately adjust** some components of your program.

4. **Adjust considerably** with a new strategy or base of information from the buyer/market.

5.   **Completely change** (greatest adjustment) your strategy because your performance is a flop. Go completely back to the table, and challenge every assumption for your next round of action.

*Sales***Minds** *increase their timing, ranging from tiny refinements to complete change.*

STAY FRESH: ADJUST FOR DOWNTIME

This is a change in our train of thought, but you might need *more* downtime to be effective. We discussed these ideas on balance in Purpose (Chapter 2). Now don't misunderstand me. I work very hard, but I know when to chill out. It's possible that the incredible hours you may be pouring in have a point of diminishing return (where the hours are not producing quality work relative to the value of that hour if you were rested). Consider:

- Travel Service *Expedia* estimates that, due to job pressures, about 18 percent of American workers give back 19.3 billion in unused vacation time. Do you need this time with your family? Do you need to get away from the grind to reignite your inner fires? Do you need to start an exercise program when you take time off?

- The Bureau of Labor Statistics reports that about one-quarter of the nation's 130 million workers toil on Saturdays, Sundays or all weekend at their main jobs. This condition produces obvious questions for any *Sales*Mind who is one of those workers: Do you have an effective, prioritized plan? Do you need to work on your skills and actions to reduce time spent to transact business during the week? I'm always a little suspicious of the productive habits of the *Sales*Mind who works all the time.

- Duke University conducted studies that showed we have a hard time being still when our technologies have turned the world into a 24/7/365 time zone.

We have to work harder to get ahead. Do you know when to turn your cell phone off? Can you sit quietly and think, pray, or meditate? Can you read to your young child or immerse yourself in their world without your own agenda pounding you?

These examples point to a key adjustment area: your work/personal life balance. I believe the healthiest *Sales*Mind has a lifestyle that reflects that they know when to be *on* and when to be *off*.

A vital but little known fact: the stress of a high-pressure job is rarely fatal. Instead, as several scientific studies have proven, the more common killing agent is job stress that is not regularly relieved by time off for rest and relaxation. When highly stressed people take time off and really put work concerns out of their minds (while they recharge their batteries), they are unlikely to suffer ill effects from prolonged job stress. Only when they fail to balance the high pressure of work and responsibility with the low pressure of rest and recreation do people place themselves at great risk of falling victim to one or more of the serious health hazards usually attributed to simple job stress.

Keep your timing fresh by (potentially) adjusting in more downtime as an investment in the quality of your uptime.

Adjustment is the *change* of timing and our last *Sales*Mind element. It is the both the daily awareness and the corrective actions that success demands. Your adjustments, together with your priorities, control of information, and coverage, are interlocking variables that will maximize your life and income opportunities within limited time.

Living and conducting business successfully certainly creates a strong calling for those *Sales*Minds willing to pay the price. Do I have to convince you of this? Probably not, because I already know you are a *Sales*Mind. How do I know? Because you've stayed with my ideas throughout this entire book, and I've tried my best to offer a contribution you would both value and enjoy.

Now the journey of this book concludes, but really it only begins again every day. So I say, good-bye for now, and press on—you're worth it.

AFTERWORD

Now the ball is in your court—the ball of transforming change. I define that change as the distance between where you are at this moment and the maximized performer you desire to be.

The experience of being a *Sales*Mind is a constant, energized condition that is both highly rewarding and at the same time, an unrelenting challenge. The powerful rewards of your new identity are a maximized income, top achievement in your field, determined confidence in your abilities, and the sincere respect and appreciation of your customers and associates. I can't imagine a business professional alive that doesn't want those identities.

But what I've learned in over twenty years of selling, training, and consulting is that being a *Sales*Mind is also a daily challenge. The challenge is keeping the concepts alive with focus and constancy of thought. Then the greatest challenge of all presents itself: applying and doing the strategies in real situations where you must deliver the proper words, under pressure, and where there is money on the line. The goal of the *Sales*Mind is not to be a book, it is to be a behavior—a daily methodology of action.

And that challenge has phases. In your early development, your task is to hungrily read and reread the concepts. Highlight them. Compare them to your current level of skill. Prioritize the concepts in relation to what you need to develop now. If you are a sales veteran, your challenge has some other dimensions. No doubt you will have had various sales training experiences over the years. The task here is to integrate the pillars of The *Sales*Mind into the fabric of your performance. Let go of your ego, and let the concepts weave themselves into the structure of your sales experience. The *Sales*Mind will ultimately settle into the role of a principled foundation for your thoughts, emotions, and efforts.

Now I have a request. I have seen this body of work change the personal and sales lives of countless people. But I want to know about *your* success. Please email me personally at doug@dougtrenary.com and let me know how The *Sales*Mind is working for you.

Finally, I thank you and am both humbled and honored by your trust and commitment to pour through this book with a desire to be the best—the desire to be a *Sales*Mind.

God Bless!

ABOUT THE AUTHOR

Doug Trenary is a unique, cutting-edge, and authoritative voice on possessing the necessary skills for personal and business success in today's competitive world.

Forget theories. After starting quickly on a success track as both a college basketball player and honor graduate, Doug took on one of the toughest sales jobs possible: selling copiers on straight commission and paying his own expenses. He made at least twenty cold calls per day selling copiers for one of America's most respected sales companies, Lanier Worldwide, racked up over 25 sales and management awards in three short years, and set records as a salesman and manager unequalled in his time.

Amazed at the fast and powerful effect training had on him, Doug became consumed with a new goal: helping others perform. At the age of 25, he founded his own training company, and since 1985, tens of thousands of people all over North America have enjoyed the warmth, humor, and passion of Mr. Trenary's corporate seminars. He has been a performance consultant and trainer to executives and sales people of such companies as Canon, MetLife, REMAX, Ryder, Sherwin Williams, ADP, and Honeywell, as well as hundreds of small businesses.

The *Sales*Mind, first created as a powerful seminar program, has evolved from Doug's real-world experience and research into the most powerful profile of today's sales achievers available anywhere. His clients have sold tens of millions of dollars by using its power in their companies.

Mr. Trenary is active in his community and church, and lives in Atlanta, GA with his wife and two children.

BRING *SALES*MIND POWER INTO YOUR COMPANY

Doug Trenary is a proven author, consultant, and powerful speaker and can contribute to your organization as an advisor or at your next event.

Some of his programs include:

- Motivational presentations for meetings and conventions.
- Sales management and executive training.
- Custom training program production for sales, management, and service.
- A full array of training and development products, including The *Sales*Mind 6-CD audio set and bulk purchases of this book.

For more information on pricing and availability of Doug Trenary's programs and products, visit www.dougtrenary.com or contact us at 1-800-578-2485 or info@dougtrenary.com.

The best is yet to come!